THE CONSUMERS' VIEW OF
FAMILY THERAPY

The Consumers' View of Family Therapy

David Howe

Gower

Published by
Gower Publishing Company Limited
Gower House
Croft Road
Aldershot
Hants GU11 3HR
England

Gower Publishing Company
Old Post Road
Brookfield
Vermont 05036
USA

British Library Cataloguing in Publication Data

Howe, David, *1946*–
    The consumers' view of family therapy.
    1. Welfare work. Family therapy
    I. Title
    362.8'286

ISBN 0 566 05793 X

Printed and bound in Great Britain at
The Camelot Press plc, Southampton

Contents

Acknowledgements

Four groups of people were of considerable help in the construction of this book and I should like to thank each of them. The family therapists were unstintingly cooperative and looked after me particularly well. My only fear is that, as a guest, I have failed to obey the usual social niceties. Typically, they have forgiven me although I am still not sure how to repay their generosity and kindness. As family therapists their practice has developed and moved on since the days of this study, in small part as a result of the research and in large part as a consequence of their own energy and commitment, and they scarcely recognize much of what is recorded in these pages. Thirty-two families allowed me – a complete stranger – to enter their homes, tape recorder in hand, curiosity to the fore. They gave me much of their time and even more of their experience. There were moments when my enthusiasm waned but some timely words of encouragement from colleagues at the University of East Anglia and Professor Phyllida Parsloe of the University of Bristol revived my flagging zeal. However, I am bound to add the usual caveat that the ideas developed in this book are my own responsibility and do not necessarily reflect the views of those who gave such welcome support. And, finally, I must thank my two children, Jacob and Rebecca, who have a touching, though hopelessly mistaken, belief that their Dad will grow rich writing academic books. Their support, not entirely unconnected with the level of their pocket money, was greatly appreciated.

David Howe
Norwich

Introduction

In 1986 three significant things happened to me. I read Hugh England's book *Social Work as Art*, I wrote a book on social work theory[1] and, most importantly, I interviewed a number of families about their experience of family therapy. Together these events acted as a powerful reminder that social work is about people – people not as clients defined by statute, not as instances of those whose social behaviour has gone astray, not as objects of scientific attention, but people as human beings who think and feel, assess and experience, suffer and celebrate. I rediscovered ideas, philosophical, sociological and literary, that placed the individual as subject (and not object) at the centre of the social stage.

It was my meetings with the families which had the greatest personal impact. I had been invited to look at the effects of family therapy on families who had approached the social services seeking help. I glimpsed how events appeared through their eyes. I saw social work from their point of view. Often the interviews would be moving occasions and I would drive home in reflective mood. For a long time social workers have recognized that the family is an important group for both understanding individual behaviour and treating certain social problems. The advent of family therapy represents a particular, but highly refined, method of working with families. It has developed a sophisticated and well articulated technology; it uses techniques which are clear, imaginative and fully rehearsed; its practitioners are enthusiastic and committed, keen to learn and eager to develop new and more effective ways of working. Inevitably, and understandably, social workers in social services and social work departments, holding a clear policy brief to see the family as a significant entity, found family therapy irresistible. It provided a sharp practical tool to complement a popular political strategy.

My research method sought the personal experiences of each family and its members. I wanted their views of family therapy. The research method assumes that the subjective experience of the individual is fundamentally important in gaining an understanding of personal and social meaning. As a form of enquiry, it has major humanistic sympathies.

Thus we have the ingredients of a classic confrontation:

technologically sophisticated practice meets humanistically-inspired investigator. The reader may wish to take sides at this point, but I have to warn him or her that the battle, though perhaps not fixed, is certainly loaded. The research style values the personal, the subjective and the experiential, which are alien concepts to the scientifically informed therapist. It may seem unfair to choose weapons that are not understood, or in fact may not even be recognized, by one of the combatants, but as the book unfolds it will become clear that one of the major sub-plots is indeed the nature of this strange relationship between the scientific practitioner on the one hand and the researcher with humanist leanings on the other. This point needs strong and early emphasis. The language and the outlook of the consumer and the researcher who reports her view may not only fail to coincide with those of the therapist, for the therapist, operating in a different universe of meaning, may simply take the consumer's view as further evidence of the family's pathological condition. In reporting what a small number of families said about their experience of therapy, I am raising a debate not only about the respective views of the consumer and the producer, but more fundamentally about the nature of evidence by which to judge a piece of social practice.

It is necessary to point out that the family therapists did not set out to do what many of the families said they did not do or felt that they should do. Thus, those families who criticized family therapy did so in terms which were never part of the therapists' practice intentions. This would be like the motor mechanic who adjusts the mixture and timing of the ignition in order to get a smooth running engine and then is criticized by the driver for being uncommunicative and not wishing to hear how upset she has been over her ailing motor. It was never the intention of the mechanic to offer a friendly, sympathetic service. Such consumer criticism appears to have no bearing on either the nature of the problem or the manner of its resolution. Whether this analogy can transfer to the arena of family work, where the engine and the driver are one and the same entity, is another matter, but at this stage it is important to appreciate that the family therapist appears to have a strong case that she is being castigated for failing to do what it was never her intention to do. She is trying to help families function smoothly. She believes that she has a set of theories and techniques that are capable of returning family systems to more effective levels of behaviour. Her case will be examined in more detail in Part III, but until then I shall present the relatively one-sided views of those who are in possession of a poor-performance family and who have little idea about the interactional mechanisms that underpin their social unit.

The encounter between the scientific practitioner and the humanistic researcher develops through three stages, each identified by the main divisions of the book. Part I outlines the rise of family therapy as an important method in childcare and social work. This is followed by an introduction to family therapy itself in which I hope to explain the underlying theory and the techniques which are based upon it.

Part II reports what a small number of families said about family therapy. It is at this point that the first blood is spilt. The families are not representative. In fact it is not the claim or the purpose of the research method to seek representativeness in terms of the types of family therapy available, the range of psychiatrists, psychologists and social workers practising this or other therapies, or the kinds of families who turn up at social services or child guidance clinics. In exploring how families perceived one group of therapists, no matter how good or bad others may feel their practice to be, it becomes possible and appropriate to map the experiential contours of a particular therapeutic technique. As a qualitative researcher, I would argue that it would be inappropriate for people to react defensively to any harsh words that families may utter. I would counsel 'let us hear what these people have to say; let us try and understand what they are trying to tell us and reflect on what it is that we think we hear'. The study is a record of 32 families and their experiences of the family therapy practised by six social workers. Out of the views expressed by the families emerge ideas and concepts that not only apply to their experience, but transfer to other situations. As I shall attempt to claim, some themes appear to have universal interest for psychiatrists, psychologists and social workers who work with children and their families. I am not looking for causal relationships between the actions of the worker and the behaviour of the client. I am exploring the meanings that a group of participants gave to a particular experience. I wish to understand this experience rather than explain individual behaviours.

Part III brings Parts I and II face-to-face. As I have said, the exchanges are unequally balanced. The analytical insights and theoretical concepts favour the qualitative researcher. However, I do give the family therapist an escape clause. She can simply refuse to recognize the grounds on which the conflict is being fought and leave the arena believing that she is unscathed. This generous offer is not made in a fit of conscience about some of the damage I may otherwise inflict. Rather it is a gesture towards those who do not like to see unfair play, and unfair play would certainly be the case if the reader and the therapist were unaware of the author's theoretical and methodological bias. But having allowed the wary reader to leave us at this stage or at least recognize what I am up to, the last third of the book discovers two important, albeit fashionable, notions; client subjectivity and consumer empowerment. These are held to be valuable ideas which have serious implications for those who wish to practise family therapy with systemic integrity. Stealing the words of Harris and Webb (1987 p. 6), the book is neither a straightforward research report nor a simple practice handbook but rather a theoretical exploration which uses the experiences of a small number of consumers as a vehicle for identifying some of the major issues that lie beneath much of current child care and family work.

Note
1. D. Howe, *An Introduction to Social Work Theory*, (Aldershot, Gower/Wildwood, 1987).

PART I

SOCIAL WORKERS AND FAMILY THERAPY

1 The rise of family therapy

Introduction

To be interested in the well-being and the proper development of children is said to require an equal interest to be taken in their families. In this sense, childcare work is family work. The state of the family is taken to be an indicator of the condition of the child and vice versa. This relationship has long been recognized but, over the last few decades, it has received much sharper conceptual, political and professional attention. Local authority social workers, acting as childcare agents, have found their responsibilities increasingly defined and understood in terms of working with families.

Family therapy is a particular and specific way of working with families. However, the growing appreciation of the importance of the family in childcare policy and practice does not explain why family therapy in particular has become so popular and widespread amongst social workers. To understand the reasons for this popularity we need to look at a number of other trends whose coincidence has allowed the practice of family therapy in social services departments to seem desirable, natural and almost inevitable. These trends are, in fact, better described as climates of understanding, ideas about what is good thinking, useful knowledge and effective practice for social workers and their organization. The interplay of these ideas amplifies certain areas of knowledge and understanding. They swell and seem to address the issues that confront departments and their workers in ways which feel direct and highly relevant. We might therefore consider the rise of family therapy in social services departments in relation to three intellectual moods:

1. The family as the focus of welfare policy and practice;
2. Scientific approaches to practice as the only way to improve professional effectiveness; family therapy as an applied science;
3. The demand that departments and social workers clarify and define their roles and purposes, methods and tasks much more vigorously in order to improve efficiency, effectiveness and economy; managerialism in social services.

The family and welfare policy

Throughout the 1950s pressures were placed on governments to inquire into the conditions of neglected children. In 1956 the Committee on Children and Young Persons (the Ingleby Committee) was set up to review juvenile justice and whether local authorities should 'be given new powers and duties to prevent or forestall the suffering of children through neglect in their own homes'. In 1960 the Committee reported, and many of its recommendations subsequently found their way into the Children and Young Persons Act, 1963. However, the Committee also noted that many of the problems found in working with children emanated from the fragmentary nature of the personal social services. They needed a concept around which to unify both how problems and needs should be defined and how welfare responses should be organized. The family proved to be such a concept. The Report announced that 'It may be that the long-term solution will be in a reorganisation of the various services concerned with the family, and their combination into a unified family service . . .' (para. 47).

A few years later, the Labour government's White Paper *The Child, The Family and the Young Offender* (1965) revived the recommendation of the Ingleby Committee to consider a unified family service. Although the White Paper itself received a hostile reception, its proposal that a 'small independent committee' be established 'to review the organisation and responsibilities of the local authority personal social services and consider what changes are desirable to ensure an effective family service' (para. 7) was viewed more sympathetically. It was this which led to the setting up, in 1965, of the Committee on the Local Authority and Allied Social Services, chaired by Frederic Seebohm. The Committee reported in 1968, and most of its main proposals were enacted in the 1970 Local Authority Social Services Act which led, a year later, to the formation of Social Services Departments in England and Wales.

The Seebohm Report represented a significant milestone in the philosophy, organization and practice of social work and the delivery of welfare services. It urged that no longer should clients be viewed within a 'symptom-centred approach', rather they should be seen as part of the family and community. Such conceptual moves meant that not only was the state responding to the family and its needs, but by approaching 'social distress' with such familial philosophies in mind it was also creating a definition of the family itself. The family became the site of important social and moral events, the outcome of which had a direct bearing on society. In placing such responsibilities with the family, the state was asserting an interest in its functioning as well as creating a view of what family life was, and should be, about.

The concept of a 'community and family oriented service' also emphasized preventative work. As well as providing a service that simply reacted to the plight of individual children, the new department and its workers could forestall the irretrievable breakdown of family life. This would entail working with families in order to prevent children coming into care, a practice which continued the philosophy of the 1963 and 1969 Children and Young Persons Acts. Moreover, the hope was that such services would be available to all families who were seeking help and advice and not just those whose children had come to the notice of the authorities. The Seebohm Report also envisaged such services being delivered by social workers who were experts in family matters: 'no really effective family service is possible unless the staff receive a sound basic training followed by opportunities to develop their skill in the light of new knowledge and changed circumstances.' The support of the family therefore became a major goal of both political policy and professional practice.

Thus, social work in the 1970s and 1980s was well placed to view the family as (i) an acceptable entity of welfare concern, (ii) an appropriate context for understanding individual behaviour, and (iii) a proper subject for professional attention.

Family therapy as an applied science
Although originally put in rather undifferentiated global terms, the question 'Is social work effective?' for a long time received the answer 'No, it is not'. In the 1950s and 1960s, the practice of social workers was still largely informed by theories which saw individual problems as a product of past emotional experiences, particularly those set in early childhood. The promotion of insight and the maturation of emotional behaviour, necessary in order to prevent inappropriate 'acting-out' of psychological conflict and anxiety, required long-term treatment. The relationship with the social worker was the vehicle in which this maturity could be reached. It was practices of this kind which were tested for their effectiveness – for example in work directed at juvenile delinquents and behaviourally problematic young children. But if such practices were not effective, then what sort of social work would fare better?

The 'effectiveness' research of this time pushed many social workers who wanted to be effective in one or other of two directions; political radicalism or scientific rigour. Those who wished to become scientifically more disciplined set themselves a number of tasks. First, they refined the question the answer to which would tell them if they were doing things right. For example, researchers might ask which particular social work actions have what effect on specified, measurable problem behaviours? Second, and as a consequence of tightening the measures by which effectiveness is judged, social workers no longer attempted to effect changes on all fronts but instead learned to focus on particular behaviours and try to do something about them. Third, they developed regular, repeatable, sequentially structured methods of practice. Whereas psychodynamically inspired practices were good at explaining what was happening but were short on offering detailed prescriptions, the new problem-focused, task-specific and time-limited approaches seemed enticingly lucid on both theory and practice. The language and practice of these fresh developments sought to be thoroughly scientific. A problem behaviour had to be described in concrete, observable terms. The world is no more than that which can be observed. The communications that surround and determine the problem behaviour had to be recognized, described and held up for examination. The social worker, having understood the nature and context of the behaviour, could then call for specified changes in those behaviours that were sustaining the problem. He or she treated the problem by manipulating the behavioural and verbal environment.

Only by following the ways of science, so the argument went, could the social worker improve his or her effectiveness. But becoming an applied scientist requires the social worker to make certain fundamental assumptions about people, their problems and the society in which these problems occur. The problem is taken to be a property of the object or system under consideration, be this an individual or family. It is the social worker's task to identify the mechanisms that cause, provoke and maintain the problem behaviour. Having identified them, usually in terms of some theoretical outlook, the social worker, as expert, decides what actions are to be taken in order to rid the individual or family of the problem. Essentially, people are viewed as objects whose behaviour is caused by physical events, including the words and deeds of other people. The individual's behaviour is capable of an objective explanation and this explanation has no need to refer to the subjective experience of those under consideration. What people say and do, rather than what they intend or mean, provides sufficient evidence on which to develop diagnoses and apply treatments.

Most brands of family therapy have been developed in the fields of psychology and psychiatric medicine. Practitioners in these disciplines have tended to look to the natural and applied sciences for inspiration. Along with many other social scientists they were particularly drawn to one area of interest and way of thinking: systems theory. Problems met in biology and ecology, cybernetics and information technology encouraged researchers to look at any entity as a system of interrelated, interconnected and interdependent parts. The whole system, be it a living creature, a tropical forest or an intricate machine, could not be understood solely in terms of adding together its constituent elements. The whole was not only more than the sum of its parts, the parts were more than a simple fraction of the whole. The overall performance and character of the system could only be understood by appreciating the relationship between the parts themselves, and, just as importantly, the relationship between the parts and the whole. This conceptual address appealed to those social scientists who liked to see social life as a particularly complex kind of system, but one which is nevertheless directly analogous to systems met in the world of nature and machines. In fact, nature and machines acted as models for explaining a variety of social 'systems'. The family was one such system. Within it, individual members both affect the overall operation of the system and in turn are affected by the system as a whole. This formulation held great attractions for many of those working with and trying to understand family life. It seemed that viewing the family as a system in its own right provided a powerful conceptual and practical tool by which to find some order and regularity in a situation that was otherwise in danger of making little sense.

However, before we elaborate the work of the family systems theorists in the next chapter, it will be helpful to give a brief history of family therapy. The works of Broderick and Schrader (1981) and Nuttall (1985) are a great help here. There were a number of precursors to the more full-blown models of family therapy found in the early 1950s both in America and the United Kingdom. Traditional psychoanalytic practices housed the first moves towards working with the family, and particular mention might be made of John Bell in the United States and John Bowlby in England. However, it was a few years later that the biggest strides occurred in taking the family, rather than the individual member, as the unit of therapeutic attention.

Originally a child psychiatrist, Ackerman became convinced that an individual's emotional problems could be understood in the context of his immediate environment. A disturbed psyche was itself the product of a disturbed social environment. He began to experiment with interviewing the whole family and, by 1958, he had published his first book on the treatment and diagnosis of family relationships, *The Psychodynamics of Family Life*. But perhaps the most potent and revolutionary force to appear at this time was assembled in what came to be known as the Palo Alto Group based at the Mental Research Institute in San Francisco. There were four founding members: Bateson, Haley, Weakland and Jackson. Bateson's background lay in anthropology and philosophy where he developed an interest in social systems and general systems theory. Haley was concerned with the nature of communication. Weakland started out as an engineer but later turned his attentions to anthropology. The exotic interplay of systems theory, anthropology and communications coupled with an active interest in the therapeutic techniques of Milton Erickson generated the basic framework in which families might be understood and treated.

When the original Rockefeller Foundation grant ran out, the team narrowed its focus and chose to examine the occurrence of schizophrenic behaviour as a specific response to a prevailing family situation. In 1954 the group secured a Macy Foundation grant. Jackson, a psychiatrist who had been working with schizophrenics, joined the team and although each member brought a distinct dimension to understanding family life, again it has to be noted that the main roots of each lay in the natural and medical sciences. The resulting practice has come to be known as the 'strategic approach'.

The group explored the relationship between schizophrenic behaviour and the pattern of communication within the patient's family. In 1956, Bateson, Jackson, Haley and Weakland developed their ideas on communication and proposed the notion of a 'double bind' in an article entitled 'Towards a Theory of Schizophrenia'. The apparently 'bizarre behaviour of a patient was seen as a response to repeated paradoxical messages received from an important, survival figure (usually a mother) which were inescapable in the patient's family' (Nuttall, 1985, p. 3). The advance made by Bateson was to suggest that the fault did not lie with the individual but with the logic of interactions in the family network. So, whereas traditional theories considered intrapsychic events, Bateson and his colleagues sought to interpret social interactions. And while, for example, Freud's theory led to individual therapy aimed at the patient's unconscious, Bateson's theory led to family therapy aimed at the communicational patterns of the group (Poster, 1978, p. 115). The great theoretical and therapeutic moves were from the psychic interior to the social exterior; from the vertical depths of mental phenomena to the horizontal surface of interpersonal exchanges.

Many key concepts received their first airing in the group's early publications. But such exciting ideas soon spilled beyond the rather specialized focus on schizophrenia. The notion that what was happening within the family system as a whole could have profound consequences for the behaviour of one particular member of that system introduced a promising new way in which to understand and work with an alleged individual problem; family therapy. Lidz, for example, was able to suggest that problems between parents might well express themselves in the behaviour of a 'problem' child. Marital conflict, delinquency, the difficult behaviour of young children and many neuroses could now 'make sense' in terms of the patterns of communication that circulated within a family system. Many features of modern-day systemic family therapies trace their history to the work of these influential pioneers.

In 1967 Haley left California, moved east and joined Minuchin at the Philadelphia Child Guidance Clinic. Together, they added a number of important techniques to the growing repertoire of the family therapist, but one of their most significant contributions – 'structural' family therapy – first saw the light of day in the early 1970s. Families provide structures which allow members to carry out their familial and social functions. In this model, parents are expected to act as parents to their children and not as friends or siblings or lovers. Children, if they are to have the opportunity to develop appropriate and acceptable social and emotional behaviours, must be allowed to be children and not be encouraged to act, for example, as parents. The problem of the 'parental child' is classic; the child assumes a parent-like responsibility and attitude towards his or her brothers and sisters. When parents are not being parents or children are not being children, the structure of the family is said to be awry and in need of treatment.

We shall enlarge upon some of these treatments in the next chapter, but at this stage we simply confirm the influence that science and some of its models had on the thinking and practice of family therapy. The practitioner was cast in the role of expert. The encounter between worker and family was steered in the direction of treatment. Mechanisms were sought to account for the operations of normal family life, deviations from which resulted in malfunctioning. Problems in the functioning of a family could be deduced from the behaviour of individual members. In particular, the unhappy, improper or odd behaviour of children provided an accurate indicator of the health of family life. The introduction of a scientific and clinical outlook into an arena that had pre-viously seemed impenetrable brought a growing enthusiasm and confidence to childcare and family work. The promise of so much control and manageability in such turbulent waters proved irresistible.

Managerialism

The vast increase in the size of personal social services organizations throughout the 1970s was accompanied by the rise of the social services manager (Howe, 1986, pp. 141–57). Learning lessons from their industrial and commercial counterparts, social services managers introduced rational planning into welfare bureaucracies. Uncertainty and raggedness in the conduct and direction of operations are anathema to managers. As much of front-line practice seemed to possess both these characteristics, good management meant that either social workers had to learn to practise in an efficient, effective and economic way or managers would impose a crisper set of operating procedures in order to standardize the organization's 'service responses'. If the latter strategy was adopted, a large element of professional self-control over the content of practice would be lost by the social worker. This has indeed been the fate of much professional work in social services departments which is now prescribed, practised and resourced according to managerial design. However, not all work is amenable to such central definition and control. If social workers themselves can find and develop techniques that make front-line practice sharper, tighter and more systematic, they are likely to earn the support of managers.

Several new theoretical and technological innovations are now available to social workers in the field of childcare and family work. They suit the needs of both practitioners and managers. Task-centred casework, behavioural approaches and caseload management techniques all capture the operating spirit of the modern welfare organization. The adjectives used to describe the various types of family therapy also have a good purposeful ring to them: systemic, strategic and structural. What all these theories and practices provide is a clear brief which requires that the social worker assume firm and confident control of the encounter between practitioner and client. Most of the techniques are problem-focused, task-centred and time-limited. This is the stuff of good organizational behaviour. Everyone – worker, client and manager – knows where they are, where they are going and how long they will be together. Thus, in the face of managerial demands to have practice look purposeful, tidy and smart, family therapy has a head start inheriting, as it does, a missionary zeal to bring clinical discipline to the problems of human relationships within troubled and troublesome families.

The formation of family therapy

Several 'theorists' of the family, usually coming from a sociological direction, have developed the view that expert interventions are not designed in response to the patterns of family life, but that the patterns of family life are 'constructed' in response to expert interventions. Morgan (1985) offers an attractive version of this thesis and in turn he makes use of the work of several other theorists including Foucault and Donzelot. The position is provocative and lies well outside the climate of thought generated within the world of family therapy. It sees the family and those who seek to treat it being shaped by various social and political cross-currents; the attitude of the state to children and their families, the medicalization of human affairs, and the way in which public concerns arise and receive social definition. This final section presents a summary of this position whose proponents seek to understand the family as an entity defined by the practices which surround and enmesh it. They do not see the family possessing essential, timeless qualities. This is how Donzelot, in characteristically tortuous fashion, describes his approach:

> The method we have employed [posits] the family, not as a point of departure, as a manifest reality, but as a moving resultant, an uncertain form whose intelligibility can only come from studying the system of relations it maintains with the sociopolitical level. This requires us to detect all the political mediations that exist between the two registers, to identify the lines of transformation that are situated in that space of intersections. (1979, p. xxv)

The family stands at the intersection of the private and the public (Morgan, 1985, p. 19). It occupies a space in which interpersonal concerns are played out before a political audience. The condition of family life is not a private matter and what goes on within families is of fundamental interest to society. The current wisdom is that many social problems arise out of the faulty workings of family life: juvenile delinquency; neglect of the very young; psychological disturbance in children. However the flow of responsibility, and therefore blame, is all one-way. Whereas difficulties in the family lead to social problems, social problems in the form of structural and economic inequalities are less likely to be seen as causing family troubles. Furthermore, the proper socialization of children to be effective citizens, economically and behaviourally, depends on the proper functioning of family life. But who defines 'proper functioning?' And what are the origins of these standards for good family relationships?

The measures and expectations that surround family living are not only held by experts but permeate the thinking and practices of families themselves. Families judge themselves and are judged by others in terms that require them to look inwards and examine the condition of their own interpersonal relationships. All this represents a shift in the concept of the family away from an institution which encompasses economic and reproductive tasks to one which represents a set of personal *relationships*. The quality of relations is taken as the main defining characteristic of a successful marriage and well-functioning family. When problems occur it is no longer the priest who is sought but the therapist. The idea that a family is a set of relationships has become the central plank for therapeutic interventions. This transformation of the family into a set of relationships detached from the economic and reproductive sphere made it amenable to science and its techniques. Science arrives in the form of medicine and the object of its concern is the interplay of human relations. We are describing, in Morgan's terms, the 'medicalisation of marriage and the family':

> In the first place, the medical model implies that there exists some class of problems called 'marital problems', that is a class of problems related to the marital relationship in some strong sense and which can, therefore, be relatively isolated for examination and treatment. . . . To treat a class of problems called 'marital problems' is to recognise or endorse the centrality of a particular definition of marriage within society of as a whole. (Morgan, 1985, pp. 34–5)

The experts seek to help those who are experiencing problems with their family relationships. However, they do more than merely respond in their attempts to treat the problems; they define and delimit the problems as 'relational' in the first place. The therapist conceives matters in such a way that family problems are approached in terms of relationship difficulties amongst family members, and are thus amenable to the skills and knowledge that the therapist brings to the situation. Having established family life as a set of interpersonal relationships that can go wrong, all behaviours are then available as possible 'symptoms' of that family's quality of relating.

As might be expected from this analysis, medical practitioners have featured prominently in the growth of family therapy, a growth which Gurman and Kniskern (1981, p. xiii) observe as being rapid. In 1970 the membership of the American Association for Marital and Family Therapy numbered 973. By 1979 it had risen to 7,565. The vocabulary and intellectual outlook of their discourse is medical and represents a way of thinking about families and the manner in which they operate. The concepts and words used reflect this orientation. Thus, we hear of aetiology and diagnosis, therapy and treatment. All family behaviours are framed within the terms of medical science. Donzelot (1979, p. 171) has a fine phrase for those who intervene in the lives of families in order to educate members and repair faults. He calls them 'technicians in human relations'.

But the therapist does not perform as a discrete operator. Behind her lies the state. The therapist, as a social agent, joins two fields of view – the judicial and the therapeutic – into one act of intervention. The state thinks of the family as a group in which parents are responsible for the welfare and developmental well-being of children. Parents, too, are responsible for the behaviour of their children so that we learn to assume that a problem child is the result of poor parenting. Thus, if parents are responsible, then parents are to blame when things go wrong. The 'parent', according to Donzelot (1979, p. 225), is continually called upon to fight against an enemy that is none other than himself. The social agent as therapist credits the family with being both the only model for socialization and the source of all dissatisfactions. The 'discourse' of the technician in human relations provides her with a subtle, though powerful cognitive hold over the family that simultaneously invades its domain yet values its existence. The family's 'margin of autonomy' is reduced 'at the same time as its internal life is in demand' (Donzelot, 1979, p. 227)

Rearing children is therefore no longer a private matter. There are notions of what family life should be like, and these are reflected in the law, in the statutory duties of health visitors and social workers, and in the intellectual yardsticks by which families are measured, explained and judged. Therapists accept this view and feel that the development of children into acceptable adults requires an environment in which the emotional and psychological relationships between members are healthy and accurate.

Donzelot's thinking is rich in a 'double-take', multi-layered imagery which can be stimulating and daring as well as elusive and irritating. For example, taking a cue from this approach, we might see the intervention of human relations experts operating at two levels simultaneously. The family is the place where children are expected to grow and develop according to established psychological principles that define healthy functioning. Departures from these principles are recognized when children fail to behave properly in the public sphere. Delinquency, truancy and poor socialization all suggest problems in the family. The logic that understands what is happening returns the 'problem' to the family, the only place that can be held responsible *and* the only place in which it can be treated. The statutory control of children and the therapeutic intervention of experts arise out of the same understanding of what the child is doing (in acts of surveillance) and what should happen to that child (in acts of education and treatment). The norms of the state enter family life. The first step is no longer to remove the problem child from the family. Instead, both 'dangerous children' and 'children in danger' are left with their families. Social agents move in. The family is the site in which to educate families on how to recover their child and how to relate in a way which will lead to good and sociable behaviour. In this way the independent authority of the family gives way to a form of social management in which the expert uses the family itself as the vehicle of change. It also follows that the family experiences an increase in supervision and intervention, direction and education. Donzelot calls all this the 'tutelary complex'.

We meet in the social worker and other therapeutic agents of the state individuals who combine treatment and teaching objectives with methods of economic and moral surveillance. This procedure, explains Donzelot (1979, p. 89), reduces the autonomy of the family. It also allows common ground to be found between aspects of the law and medicine, psychiatry and social work. Their practices define the family and in turn this definition of the family allows a new field of view to emerge which encompasses these previously disparate practices. A 'familial' explanation arises to account for a whole series of social behaviours and expectations. A 'junction' is established between the moral and the judicial; a 'homogeneous grid' emerges that sets up 'different levels of communication between parents' behaviour, the educative value of a family, the moral characteristics of children, and their pedagogical problems' (ibid., p. 149). Once alert to the child who is in danger of slipping out of social acceptability, the machinery of prevention clicks into operation. But:

> Set within this double network of social guardians and technicians, the family appears as though colonised. There are no longer two authorities facing one another: the family and the apparatus, but a series of concentric circles around the child: the family circle, the circle of technicians, and the circle of social guardians. (Donzelot, 1979, p. 103)

The social worker views the family from several perspectives simultaneously. As a 'social guardian' she is mindful of the behavioural standards of the family and its children. As an expert in family life she understands how the problematic condition arose. And as a technician in human relations she helps the family to recover an effective level of functioning. It is extremely important to recognize the combined nature of these various practices when we come to consider how the social worker is viewed by both families and social researchers. It is difficult to hold the several practices in focus at the same time. Just when you feel you have one clearly in view, it disappears and you are faced with a different one. As we shall see, families begin to feel like Alice Through the Looking Glass; things are never quite what they seem and they certainly do not behave in a fixed and constant fashion. The effect can be most disorientating. Ambiguity is built into the social worker's practice: she can be a guardian, she can be a technician and sometimes she can be both. Ambiguities, though, are likely to provoke ambivalence. This is a useful observation which we need to bear in mind, particularly when, in Part II, we come to explore what families who have been at the receiving end of therapeutic interventions have to say about their experiences.

The point being made is that the concept and practice of family life do not exist prior to these definitions and moral precepts. There is no essential quality to family life. Prevailing political, intellectual and social attitudes 'construct' the family as an entity displaying certain properties. The characteristics of the well-functioning family are a product of time and place, of ideas and intentions. However, so powerful are such current wisdoms that whatever standards they promote seem natural and obvious rather than fabricated and puzzling. In this sense, theorizing about the nature of the family is an ideological activity where ideology is seen as a set of beliefs and values which are taken to be the way things actually are – although we might equally choose to see them as just the way things currently happen to be. 'What ideology does', writes Morgan (1985, p. 295), '. . . is to select from the range of possible ways in which a society might handle the relationships between the biological and the cultural, particularly in the sphere of childbirth and parenthood, and to proclaim the method so selected as *the* method, as natural and inevitable.' Variations and deviations from such patterns of relating both account for the 'problem' and become the method by which the problem is addressed and treated.

I have deliberately spent time looking at the idea that family practices take on their shape and form as they relate to the surrounding social and political world. It is the context in which the rise of family therapy might be understood. It is certainly the context in which it is 'constructed'. As we shall see, this style of analysis, though liable to be arcane, is well worth the effort. It will help us think about social work and family therapy in some unusual but rewarding ways.

Conclusion

When a number of intellectual and political currents collect and run in the same direction, the ideas and practices which they support swell and break the social surface. It is as if their time had come. The dimensions that constitute their form are all present and so they gain shape and substance and then appear as timely and appropriate. Family therapy is defined by views which recognize the family as an important social group and which see that an individual's behaviour is effectively understood as a product of family life and interaction. Family therapy appeals to a critical range of welfare concerns. As we have seen, it appears to satisfy the interests of policy-makers, those who seek professional credibility and those who look for practices which are compatible with good organizational behaviour. Any practice that appeals to politicians, professionals and managers is likely to be irrepressible. But what is this practice? We need now to learn a little of what family therapy is, what it looks like and how it proceeds.

2 The theory and practice of family therapy

Introduction

Family therapy is not a uniform endeavour. Its practice varies according to its theoretical origins. However, over recent years by far and away the most influential sets of ideas to affect family therapy have been general systems theory and its close relative, communication theory. The literature on those treatment schools which use a 'systemic' approach is vast. It is not my purpose to review the full and varied range of these writings but rather to recognize that practices based on systems theory produce a distinctive approach to the understanding and treatment of problem behaviour within a family setting. In this chapter I shall deliberately emphasize the ingredients that characterize the intellectual make-up of this method of working. However, for those who wish to hear a fuller and less selective account of what family therapy has to offer there are a number of very readable and highly practical introductory texts now available, many of which are written with the social worker specifically in mind (for example, Burnham, 1986; Gorrell Barnes, 1984; Manor, 1984; Masson and O'Byrne, 1984; Walrond-Skinner, 1977).

Systems theory swept into social work in the 1970s. It changed the general landscape but not to the extent that those who rode in on its full flood predicted or would have liked. In social work, only family therapy retains a vigorous commitment to systems thinking. But its interest in systems theory comes less from ideas explored in welfare work and more from developments in family therapy itself, which generally emanate from the worlds of psychiatry, medicine and psychology.

As we have seen, the main conceptual breakthrough in systems thinking was the idea that many natural and mechanical systems possess properties which are more than the simple sum of their parts. Indeed, such systems can only be understood and addressed at the level at which their parts interrelate as a whole. At root, the approach is scientific insofar as systems are taken to be composed of concrete, empirical elements, the collective behaviour of which not only produces a functioning whole but also allows this behaviour to be measured by an external observer seeking to discern the inherent characteristics of the system. Elements within the system are said to relate in a regular, patterned way and it is one of the tasks of the observer to recognize and appreciate these regularities. Many behavioural and social scientists attempt to apply the models and methods of the natural sciences to the study of human affairs. The use of self-regulating mechanical and biological analogies as a means of modelling and understanding the social world is particularly favoured by applied social scientists. The ideas of Ludwig von Bertalanffy, the father of much of modern systems theory, were triggered by concerns he had in biology and engineering. He believed that the notion of a 'system' could apply to subject areas as diverse as physics and sociology, biology and information technology. The task of his General Systems Theory is to discover the principles of organization and the structural uniformities that underlie any system. Thus, the metaphor of 'system' acts as an organizing concept (Burrell and Morgan, 1979, p. 58).

Therapies which appeal to systems theory for conceptual and practical guidance make basic assumptions about the nature of human behaviour. These assumptions determine the way behaviour is understood and the manner by which it might be changed. The suggestion in Chapter 1 was that the scientific climate in which family therapists operate and which sustains their intellectual vision fundamentally colours the way in which the family is approached. The family therapist does not believe that behaviour is altered by changing feelings, meanings and experiences. Rather, she believes that feelings, meanings and experiences are changed by altering behaviour. 'Perceptions and subjective feelings', writes Stanton (1981, p. 372), 'are seen more as dependent than independent variables, since they change with changes in interpersonal relationships.' The therapist directs actions and interactions in the 'here-and-now'. She does not invite introspection. Nor does she explain the thinking which lies behind her instructions. The therapist is therefore a determinist and a positivist in her approach to social phenomena. Human behaviour is caused, albeit in a non-linear matrix of mutually interacting parts.

In the wake of these assumptions it is time to state the two main theoretical outlooks of the practitioner who subscribes to a systemic view of family functioning. First, the family is understood as a system of mutually interacting and interdependent parts. The parts only 'make sense' as constituents of the whole. Second, the level of intervention is the whole family system. Individual members have no discrete existence as far as the systemic therapist is concerned. Thinking about and acting upon families in the light of these two outlooks represents a major shift in reasoning about the causes and effects of behaviour. The individual member is not the level at which behaviour is understood or treated. Psychologies emerge out of interactional patterns. No longer is the focus on the individual character of personal psychology; rather it is on the social nature of psychic life. What goes on *between* people is more important than what goes on *within* them. For example, Murgatroyd and Woolfe (1985, p. 6) see the individual and his or her distress as a product of family processes. So, rather than speak about 'needs in terms of individuals (i.e. "Jack's a very depressed person" or . . . "Mike is confused"), the family focused helper is led to speak about "the family's depression as currently shown by Jack" or . . . "the confusion Mike and others share"' (ibid., pp. 6–7). There is a distinct change in emphasis away from the state of the individual to the quality of the relationship.

> These theories, which were connected with the war, with the development of computers and with advanced capitalist society, led Bateson to emphasise communication patterns over private fantasies. The analysis of the message and the circuit required a set of concepts which made the individual intelligible only in the social matrix. All behaviour could be viewed as communication, according to Bateson, but not in terms of the intentions of the individual. Communication was a question above all of interaction and rules for interaction; meaningful words and gestures implied both a sender and a receiver. In sum, communication was intelligible not from the point of view of the individual but only in the context of a relation. (Poster, 1978, p. 111)

There is a move from simple linear cause and effect (John's behaviour is the cause of the family's troubles) to more complex and circular accounts of the relationship between causes and effects (John's behaviour causes Mum to row with Dad who takes it out on John who misbehaves which causes Mum to . . .). 'Circular causality' is an important notion in family therapy. It ranges from the simple cycle of 'he withdraws because she nags and she nags because he withdraws' to the more elaborate three-generational conflicts found, say, between a grandmother, a single parent and her child, a good example of which is given by Haley (quoted in Masson and O'Byrne, 1984, p. 11):

1. Grandmother takes care of the grandchild while protesting that mother is irresponsible and does not take care of the child properly. In this way grandmother is siding with the child against the mother in a coalition across generation lines.

2.   Mother withdraws, letting grandmother care for the child.
3.   The child misbehaves or expresses symptomatic behaviour.
4.   Grandmother protests that she should not have to take care of the child and discipline him. She has raised her children and mother should take care of her own child.
5.   Mother begins to take care of her own child.
6.   Grandmother protests that mother does not know how to take care of the child properly and is being irresponsible. She takes over the care of the grandchild to save the child from mother.
7.   Mother withdraws, letting grandmother care for the child.
8.   The child misbehaves or expresses symptomatic behaviour.

The family system is a functioning entity with inherent properties which the therapist seeks to identify objectively and explain in terms of biological or cybernetic models. However, this 'external' view of the family cannot be gained or known by individual family members who remain part of the system being observed. By systemic definition, members cannot step outside the whole of which they are a part without that whole ceasing to be that which it was. The explanatory reference point is taken to lie with the therapist. She is therefore the expert, able to identify the manner in which the family system functions. By definition, all behaviours displayed by that system are features which confirm the operating style (for good or bad) of that system. In other words, whatever a family member says or does, it has no status other than that of a property of the whole system. It has no independent meaning.

All of this places the therapist in an unusually strong position. The family is rendered intelligible in terms which are of her choosing. The therapist imposes a conceptual framework on the family to help her explain what she believes to be taking place. The family is not made aware of these explanations. In fact attempts by family members to make statements independent of the system of which they are a part are either outlawed or simply returned as further evidence of the system's operating characteristics. Many therapists go on to declare that, for the duration of each therapeutic session, they too become part of that family's system. They 'join' the family. However, they retain a privileged position insofar as only their (systemic) version of what is said to be happening counts. Unlike other members they can both experience the system and view it objectively. They can make statements (diagnoses and treatment objectives) which are independent of the system under scrutiny. It appears that therapists have their cake and eat it. But, more seriously, this general line of thought has deep implications for the status of any observation or experience that a family member may care to announce. For the therapist, each announcement can only be a further demonstration of that family's state of functioning. But what might such observations mean, for example, to a researcher who asks that member 'what did you make of family therapy?' Whereas the therapist reifies the family, the interpretive researcher takes each member's experience as discrete, personal, valid and 'meaningful'. These matters raise issues to do with what type of knowledge counts in such affairs and how is such knowledge gained. Questions of epistemology and methodology lurk behind our present enquiries but, having given them an early, albeit brief airing, I shall rest them a while, revive them momentarily at the end of this chapter and then give them a final rousing in Part III.

General Systems Theory: communication theory and family therapy

The potential diagnostic and therapeutic power of seeing the family as a particular instance of a complex system became apparent to many workers in the field in the 1950s. Although the family could not be viewed as a closed system (for it had to deal with the world outside in order to survive), it did offer an unusual example in which members spent a large part of their lives together as a unit, the existence of which helped maintain the members (physically and psychologically) as well as being maintained by those members itself. General Systems Theory has generated a large number of important analytical concepts, although not all of them apply with equal force or relevance to the family system. I shall mention just a few that have been of particular use to family therapy.

The concepts of *homeostasis* and *feedback* underpin the rational analysis of any system. Homeostasis, at its simplest, means 'same state'. How do systems maintain themselves in a constant and steady state? What do they need to happen both inside and outside the system in order to keep going as a viable entity? Questions such as these can be asked of living organisms, self-regulating machines, or families. 'Homeostasis', writes Walrond-Skinner (1977, p. 14), 'is made possible by the use of information coming from the external environment and being incorporated into the system in the form of "feedback". Feedback triggers the system's "regulator", which by altering the system's internal condition, maintains homeostasis.' The favourite example given at this point is that of the thermostat mechanism in a heating system. The fuel is burnt and so the temperature rises to a pre-fixed point. A heat-sensitive mechanism or thermostat recognizes when that point is reached. This information is fed back to the fuel-burner in the form of an electrical message which says 'switch-off'. The temperature then falls and the thermostat stops sending the 'switch-off' message. This causes the heat generator to re-ignite, and so on. Homeostatis is therefore a self-correcting mechanism, one which offers important insights into family functioning – the ways in which families develop habits, often unconscious, that help maintain their particular way of life. The way in which a family deals with a need or difficulty may either promote its well-being (in which case it is said to be functional) or it may maintain or exacerbate its problems (in which case it is described as dysfunctional). According to the principle of homeostatis, systems have an in-built resistance to change (Masson and O'Byrne, 1984, p. 7). Walrond-Skinner gives an example:

> A family is faced with several external threats to its survival, such as an acute physical illness in mother and unemployment in father. Mother has to be hospitalised for a period and father has to find a new job. The family would need the assistance of homeostatic mechanisms to 'regulate' it in this crisis situation and might, for example, require the eldest daughter to take over some of mother's practical and emotional functions during her absence. She might need to be more 'maternal' to her younger siblings and more supportive and companionable to her father in his own insecurity. In this situation, the daughter's role changes would act as useful homeostatic mechanisms. However, if, when mother returned to health and father became well established in his new job, difficulties began to appear in the marital relationship, these original homeostatic mechanisms, far from alleviating the new problem, might well create secondary problems in themselves. Unfortunately, however, because of the daughter's role changes had proved a useful means of combating the original external threats posed to the family system, the homoeostatic mechanisms might actually start to *overfunction*. Rather than returning to her previous emotional position within the family and allowing her father and mother to re-integrate their relationship as husband and wife, the daughter becomes agoraphobic, refusing to relinquish her role as 'mother' and 'housewife'. . . . In this situation, the daughter, as an identified agoraphobic patient, then puts up a smokescreen in front of the marital relationship and, by concentrating the family's energy and attention on herself, she, on the one hand, prevents the marital difficulties from becoming explosive, but also prevents husband and wife from working on their difficulties in a way which would bring about some fundamental resolution. (1977, pp. 15–16)

So far I have emphasized that the family is a system of interacting parts. But the currency of that interaction is *communication* – both verbal and non-verbal. In communication, information is exchanged. 'Information exchange implies the concept of a mutually affecting process between components and involves the notion of feedback' (Walrond-Skinner, 1977, p. 17). Communication is never linear and one-way. It circulates, becomes transformed and can be compounded in a spiralling series of exchanges. The concept of a 'double-bind' identified by the Palo Alto Group was an early attempt to examine how communications could produce problems. The focus of attention was on the communication pattern within a family. In particular, it was noted that contradictory messages by parents to a child could have a confusing, disorganizing effect on the mental condition of that child, causing a serious psychological disturbance. All behaviour is a form of communication. It is therefore impossible not to communicate. Even silence will carry a message and it will certainly receive some kind of interpretation. Systemic therapists are very alert to the nature, direction and quality of the communications that circulate within a family. They are keen to spot what pieces of information are going where and with what effect.

Beyond these basic conceptual orientations lie a range of treatment schools. Each emphasizes some favoured dimension of the family system and the relationship therein. Social workers tend to plunder and adapt a number of these approaches, but the final products look broadly similar. A very good 'hybrid' is the systemic approach devised by Burnham (1986) and described in his clear and readable book on family therapy. It speaks directly to social workers interested in the technique. He draws on the four main methods: Minuchin's structural family therapy, Haley's strategic approach, The Mental Research Institute's (Palo Alto Group) brief therapy and the Milan Association's style of systemic therapy led by Palazzoli. The result seems to suit the organizational setting in which social workers usually find themselves. It also appears to fit the needs of social work's clientele. The hybrid formulation declares that 'problems are viewed as parts of repetitive sequences of interaction which maintain and are maintained by the problem ... Practitioners using a systemic approach *aim to identify and change the meaning and functioning of a presenting problem* within the context of such a system' (Burnham, 1986, p. 7 (my emphasis)). This style of intervention is met throughout all branches of systemic therapy. It is deliberately directive and direct. It is unavowedly treatment-orientated. As Aponte and VanDeusen state in their discussion of structural family therapy:

> The goals of family therapy are to solve problems and change the underlying systemic structure. The structural family therapist sees the problem to be dealt with as sustained by the current structure of the family and its ecosystem. . . . The therapist prefers to investigate what the family structures can and cannot do by intervening directly in the

transactions of the family to bring about change in the structural patterns of their sequences. (1981, pp. 315–16)

Masson and O'Byrne (1984, p. 27) also advise direct intervention, seeing it as their therapeutic 'responsibility to manoeuvre the family sub-systems into behaving in such ways as to enable, rather than hinder, satisfactory functioning'.

The systemic therapist is keenly interested in the pattern of relationships that occur within a family. Indeed, it is not her intention to change problem people but rather to change problem patterns.

> In traditional individual psychotherapy, symptoms and problematic behaviour are seen as an expression of conflicts *within* the individual; a patient might talk about 'my depression', seeing it as an expression of his/her inner world. In contrast, family therapists try to understand symptomatic behaviour within the context of the family system. (In an interview with a young couple ... Minuchin asks the wife who is complaining of depression, '*who* is depressing you?' Instead of dwelling on her feelings, he is leading her towards an interactional view of her behaviour with her husband.) (Manor (ed.), 1984, p. 10)

In terms of their *behaviours*, members of a family may relate to each other based on their differences (complementary relationships), their similarities (symmetrical relationships) or a mixture of the two (reciprocal relationships). Each one of these can be seen as either healthy or unhealthy. For example, a symmetrical relationship may be appropriate between two similarly aged children who treat each other as equals. But between a mother and grandmother, it could end up with both wishing to assume the dominant role, resulting in a never-ending series of arguments in which neither one is able to give way.

Minuchin considers the pattern of *emotional* relationships within families. *Enmeshment* describes those relationships which are extremely close, often excluding all others. This may be acceptable for a short while as in the case of lovers or a newborn baby and its mother, but it is not a good recipe for effective, long-term functioning.

> Those involved in an enmeshed relationship tend to react very quickly to small amounts of distress in their partners. Differences between people seem to be mistrusted and discouraged. A family motto might be 'all for one and one for all'. Emphasis is on loyalty, shared views, and joint activities. ... Such families often present with difficulties at times of separation and individuation (for example children might refuse to go to school). (Burnham, 1986, p. 15)

Difficulties become turned inwards and lead to disturbances in family relationships. *Disengagement* indicates distance in a relationship. The family wisdom here is 'stand on your own two feet' and 'don't get over involved' (ibid., p. 15). Members starve each other of emotional warmth with the result that tensions, in direct contrast to enmeshed families, get turned and pushed outwards on to the world in acts of delinquency and aggression.

It is common for systemic therapists to examine subsets of the whole system. For example, groups of three, or triads, often prove to be of great interest and therapeutic significance. Mothers may act as 'mediators' between fathers and step-children, or a child may become caught up in his parent's conflict. *Alliances* may develop between two members which excludes a third. *Coalitions* represent a joining of forces, usually against a third member. 'A mother may know that a child has been in trouble at school and agree not to tell the father if the child does not tell about something that she has done' (Burnham, 1986, p. 19).

Many therapists believe that *boundaries* between the generations should be clearly maintained. When these become crossed or blurred, problems arise. Treatment aims to restore such boundaries. This generally means that parents should see themselves in charge and that they should feel good and confident about this:

> The making and breaking of boundaries is a central feature of many therapists' interventions. Enmeshed families are seen as having diffuse boundaries ... while disengaged families tend to have rigid boundaries.... Health lies in having clear yet permeable boundaries.... This allows for distance to be established without losing contact, and contact to be maintained without losing individuality. (Burnham, 1986, p. 20)

Boundary problems increase at times of transition when individual family members enter new phases in their life cycle: adolescence, motherhood, marriage. If the transition is proving difficult to negotiate or accommodate, *symptoms* may emerge in members. These serve the homeostatic function of preventing change within the family. Agoraphobia is commonly explained in these terms. For example, a mother who cannot cope with her daughter's adolescent behaviour (boyfriends, rudeness and staying out late at night) may develop agoraphobia. Mother's 'problem' requires the young girl to stay home at night, give up her boyfriend, look after mum and renounce growing up. It is helpful to consider the function which the symptom serves in the family. It may be that a symptom which appears to bring distress to one member may be saving others in the family from facing severe anxieties (Manor (ed.), 1984, p. 10). 'A symptom', says Stanton (1981, p. 364), 'is regarded as a communicative act, with message qualities, which ... has a function within the interpersonal network. ... A symptom usually appears when a person is "in an impossible situation and is trying to break out of it.".' According to Murgatroyd and Woolfe:

> The symptom carrier's major role in the family is to highlight the distress the family as a whole is experiencing. Seeing the bedwetting child or the glue-sniffer as an individual with a personal problem is one option the helper has; another is to recognise the importance of that person to the family and see his or her behaviour as both personally distressing and a powerful symbol of the family's distress. (1985, pp. 55–6).

It is extremely important to remember that the therapist also represents change and that the family's normal homeostatic mechanisms will function to resist this threat. Overall, a systemic orientation towards dysfunction can be summarized as follows (Stanton, 1981, p. 365; Masson and O'Byrne, 1984, p. 122):

1. Symptoms can be viewed simply as particular types of behaviour functioning as homeostatic mechanisms which regulate family transactions. The therapist therefore has to ask 'What function does the symptom (presenting problem) serve in the family?'
2. Problems in an identified patient cannot be considered apart from the *context* in which they occur and the *functions* which they serve.
3. An individual cannot be expected to change unless his family system changes.
4. The therapist has to anticipate the consequences of change and recognize the nature and function of any resistance met.

The above examples and the concepts used to bring them into sharper relief highlight the point that the family, seen as a system, only 'makes sense' within the logic of the framework imposed. Randomness of observation is removed by seeing behaviours as part of a theoretical pattern of possible relationships, as examples of how that system conducts its exchanges of information. Thus, particular behaviours will be categorized, within the terms offered by the theory, as instances of a symptom, a coalition or enmeshment. Explaining and categorizing are the first steps towards achieving control: the flux of events can be tamed. Family therapy's ability to bring order into observation is its first great attraction to social workers. Its second is that having made sense of the situation it suggests ways of bringing about change. If the pattern of relationships is unhealthy then it must be restructured, altered and redirected towards a state of proper functioning. The therapist intervenes to restore boundaries, subvert coalitions and improve the quality of feedback. It is impossible to do justice to the full range and colour of the intervention techniques now available to the family therapist. They lack nothing in imagination and adventure. The examples given below are designed to illustrate the nature of these techniques and, once again, reveal some of the assumptions that family therapy makes about human behaviour and the treatment of family life.

Applying family therapy

The explanatory formula sees the family as a system containing a pattern of interdependent relationships. The systemic family therapist seeks to shift the balance, quality and direction of these relationships thereby changing the established operating style of that family. Gurman, Kniskern and Pinsof define family therapy as 'any psychotherapeutic endeavour which explicitly focuses on altering the interactions between or among family members, and seeks to improve the functioning of the family as a unit, the functioning of its subsystems, and/or the functioning of individual members of the family' (quoted in Johnson, 1986, p. 299). Therapeutic change comes when the 'therapist intervenes actively and directively in particular ways in a family system' (Haley, 1971, p. 7). She aims to substitute new patterns of behaviour and break unhelpful feedback loops by 'shaking up the system' (Stanton, 1981, p. 391). As much of the system's problem behaviour occurs in the form of repetitive communications that circulate between family members ('games without end'), a favourite task of the therapist is to redirect, break or 'punctuate' these ingrained patterns of behaviour. Some approaches are more aggressive in this than others. Minuchin, for example, '*joins* with a family and then *challenges* "how things are done" and then *restructures* the family by offering alternative, more functional ways of perceiving and behaving' (Burnham, 1986, p. 65).

However, before the therapist can work with the whole family, she needs to spend some time helping members appreciate the benefits of seeing everyone and not just the 'problem' individual. Families need to be motivated before they will commit themselves to therapy. The basic messages that the therapist gives are 'no-one is to blame', 'it really is very helpful to have the views of each member' and 'problems such as these are solved more quickly when the whole family is involved'. Almost from the beginning many therapists propose a *hypothesis* which holds up a possible relationship between the problem and the operating characteristics of the family's system. Through question and observation, 'acting-out' and 'sculpting', 'reconstruction' and demonstration, the hypothesis is tested. A relatively recent addition to the ways in which a systemic hypothesis may be evaluated is that of *circular questioning*:

> The theme is to gather information by asking questions in terms of differences and hence relationships. In addition to the usual direct questions, family members are asked, in turn, to comment on the thoughts, behaviour, and dyadic relationship of the other members of the family. For example, the therapist might say to the father, 'Since your mother-in-law came to live with your family has the relationship between your son and his mother been better or worse?'. . . . triadic questions should be prefaced with phrases such as 'in/your opinion', 'from your point of view', or 'from your position'. For example, 'Susan, in your opinion how do your mother and younger sister get on since your father died?' (Burnham, 1986, p. 110)

The technique helps produce a rich, dense pattern in the fabric of family relationships, adding to the evidence for or against a particular hypothesis. If a hypothesis is validated, it provides a basis for an intervention. If disproved, then another is raised for further testing until one is found to fit the behavioural pattern of the family under treatment. Again and again the aim is to build up a picture of relationships and the circular nature of interactions, to 'make patterns visible' in the 'here and now'.

Once a family's pattern of relating is recognized, the therapist is in a position to intervene. Her intervention is designed to introduce new patterns of relating. The technique of *reframing* the problem is widely used at this stage. Watzalawick *et al.* say:

> To reframe ... means to change the conceptual and/or emotional setting or viewpoint in relation to which a situation is experienced and to place it in another frame which fits the 'facts' of the same concrete situation equally well or even better, and thereby changes its entire meaning. (1974, p. 95)

By helping a family redefine the assumptions which lie beneath its usual way of doing things, family members are enabled to move out of those behaviours and fruitless exchanges that perpetuated the problem.

While interventions such as advice giving and task-setting represent direct assaults, there are indirect interventions which are famed for their cunning and subtlety. They have given family therapy some notoriety. An indirect or *paradoxical injunction* is one which the therapist expects the family to defy. According to

Palazzoli and her Milan colleagues, since the symptom is part of the family's established pattern of relating according to a fixed set of operating rules, the only way to eliminate the symptom is to change the rules. This usually calls for drastic measures. The family is forced to break its dysfunctional habits by coming face-to-face with a paradox. Cade (1984) defines paradox techniques as 'those interventions in which the therapist apparently promotes the worsening of problems rather than their removal'. A family is asked to do what everyone so far, including itself, has said they should stop doing. This has been called 'prescribing the symptom'. Of course, the therapist actually expects that the family will defy such a 'crazy' instruction and so discover that it has actually broken with a long-established rule of behaviour. The dysfunctional base that produced the symptom is dissolved and the problem behaviour disappears.

The technology of therapy
So far, two themes have run hand in hand: (i) problems in family life for so long beyond the control of social workers appear to become susceptible to more accurate diagnosis and treatment when exposed to the techniques of systemic family therapy; and (ii) systemic family therapy is a product of developments in those sciences which have addressed issues associated with complex organic, mechanical and information processing systems. There are clear methodological and stylistic consequences when these two themes are combined. Families with problems are said to demonstrate dysfunctional behaviour. The therapist is unambiguously in the driving seat; she is the expert and she determines the content, structure and direction of treatment. The logic of the encounter when therapist meets family is in the hands and head of the therapist. The family, in terms of making sense of what is going on, remains essentially passive. Pathology, positivism and power produce a clinical practice with distinctive properties, particularly when set within a welfare context.

Practising within a positivist framework, the therapist, as an applied scientist, applies her rules of interpretation, and hers only, to the encounter. As we have said, any interpretations that the family offer are either not considered or, more likely, viewed as operating characteristics of the family system. So far, in our account, we have learned how the therapist sees and tackles the world from her point of view. We have considered, albeit briefly, the kind of knowledge and assumptions she uses to make sense of people and their situation. The next step is to explore how the same encounter looks from the receiving end. What do families make of family therapy? Part II reports the findings of a small-scale study of the views and experiences of families who have undergone therapy.

We might also note that when we start to look at the world from the standpoint of the consumer, the vocabulary also changes. We begin to talk of personal experience and not observed behaviour, we look to the subject's account of what went on and not to an objective measure of a family's pattern of functioning. But what kind of knowledge does this line of enquiry provoke? Does it matter, in therapeutic terms, what the family thinks so long as it is returned to proper functioning? If family therapy provides a therapeutic structure in which the nature and locus of the problem can be understood, and if it can produce techniques capable of prising apart faulty relationships and thereby returning them to proper functioning, perhaps family therapy can be compared to the osteopath who manipulates painful out-of-joint bones, snapping them back into their correct operating position. In this case is it relevant what the family thinks of its experience? We might as well ask whether it matters what the computer thinks about the way it is repaired as long as it produces the right numbers. But of course it may matter what the computer thinks if thinking did affect the numbers produced. When the experiences of the participants themselves become a factor in the way they perform and understand themselves, we enter a more exotic world of meaning. It is simply not available to one person to hold a monopoly of what things shall mean. Epistemologically, if no one interpretation is taken as privileged, we are in for an interesting time when systemic therapist meets problem family. This is to anticipate later arguments. First we need to hear what a small number of families have to say about their experiences of therapy.

PART II

FAMILIES AND THEIR EXPERIENCE OF THERAPY

3 The family therapy team and its families

The invitation

In the spring of 1985 a group of six social workers practising family therapy in a social services department area team took an unusual but commendable decision. They sought to have their work evaluated. To this end, I was approached. Although there had been some changes of personnel, the family therapy team itself had been in existence for about three years. Over that time the workers had developed and refined their practice. It was at a stage when the team members felt it would be interesting and appropriate to have their work considered by an outsider. Quite what this might mean occupied several meetings in which we explored what they, as therapists, would like out of the exercise and what I, as a researcher, thought would be useful and interesting.

The effect of combining that which was of interest with that which might be useful suggested two evaluative measures: (i) the state of the identified problem behaviour at the end of 'treatment' *and* twelve months later; and (ii) the families' view of family therapy. The main emphasis, in time, interest and effort would, in fact, go towards understanding the consumers' experience. As little is known about the experience and perceptions of families receiving therapy in a social work context, it was felt that this would be a point of view worth appreciating. Consumer research has made a case that the client's view is an important one in the evaluation of a welfare service. It appeals to research strategies which value understanding the subjective experience of participants rather than measuring their objective behavioural condition. It describes itself in qualitative, and not quantitative, terms and it is liable to call its methods 'interpretive' rather than scientific or empirical. Understanding people's experience of family therapy was taken to be relevant to social workers and their practice.

The research method

All families who either had been offered family therapy but not accepted it as a treatment method or had completed a course of family therapy within the twelve month period 1 July 1985 to 30

June 1986 constituted the research population. After a 'case' had been closed or the therapy had been completed, one of the department's senior managers wrote to the family asking if it would be willing to participate in the research (see the Appendix). Assurances were given that the researcher was independent of the agency and that the views of the family, though reported, would remain anonymous.

As many of the problems brought by the families were both sensitive and fraught in nature, a number of strategies were employed to encourage participation in the research. A small fee was payable in recognition of the time given to the research interview. Each family was asked to contact the senior manager if it did not wish the researcher to visit. If the senior manager did not hear from the family within a specified time, it would be assumed that it was happy about the proposed visit. In total the department wrote to 34 families. Only two preferred not to be interviewed. One had been offered family therapy but had not accepted. The other had accepted treatment but walked out in the middle of the first session and did not return. As the researcher, I then contacted the willing families and booked a convenient time to see them in their own homes. In a number of cases it was necessary to clarify further who I was and what I was up to. A few families thought I was about to give them a supplementary dose of therapy until I reiterated the purpose of my visit. All the families were happy about the proposed interview being audio-tape recorded. Because it was important to engage their interest and cooperation, I was very careful to give a full description of (i) the purpose of the research; (ii) the method of the research; and (iii) the destination of their comments and observations (in the form of a written report available to the family therapy team, the social services department and the wider public).

The interviews took place between four and seven weeks after case closure or completion of treatment. In all but three cases it was possible to interview all members of the families who had been in therapy. In two of the remaining cases, two of the children (siblings of the 'identified patient') were out with friends at the time of the interview. In the third – a case of 'incest' – the parents decided that it would not be appropriate for me to see their daughter: 'she's been through enough already.'

The structure of the interviews was open-ended, although there was a rough theme which followed the families' 'story' of how they perceived their problem, how they got in touch with the social services, and how they experienced family therapy. All the families had much to say and many things to tell. Interviews with those who were offered family therapy but did not accept ranged in length between 20 and 50 minutes. The interviews with those families who had received treatment varied between 60 and 100 minutes.

I was also granted access to the detailed records made by the family therapy team after each session as well as the more usual agency files. The contents of the audio-tapes and records formed data out of which the researcher created categories of interest, common themes and analytical concepts. When reporting this data, all names have been fictionalized and details which may identify a particular family have been changed or masked to preserve anonymity.

As in much research of this nature, the aim was to gain *understanding* rather than seek explanation or identify causal relationships. In the words of Fisher *et al.* (1986, p. 19), I wanted 'to obtain a clear picture of the feelings, aspirations, hopes and fears' of those involved. The method was designed to explore how families viewed therapy and to learn how they made sense of the experience. The enquiry was interested in gaining a view that was client-based; not that such a perspective was better, but just different. If the nature of this difference could be appreciated and given expression, I felt that an extra dimension would be added to any discussion about the theory and practice of working with families. What I was after were concepts and categories that seemed to capture the experiential condition of the client.

However, I also accept that qualitative data is better described as 'interpretive research' (Bulmer, 1979, p. 673). The basic role of the qualitatively orientated researcher in the business of data collection and analysis is that of interpreter. It is not just, as Glaser and Straus (1967) argue, a case of allowing categories and concepts to emerge from the data as if what you see and hear merely surfaces as you explore the accounts which people give of their experiences. This would be a case of pure induction. Rather, what you see and hear as a researcher is influenced by some of the concepts already possessed and for which you have a predilection. However, such preliminary concepts will evolve in the light of the data gathered. Like the artist, the researcher creates an interaction with his or her medium and its properties. Again, Bulmer covers similar ground: 'Concepts ... are categories for the organization of ideas and observations' (1979, p. 652). The explicit use of concepts is one of the most important characteristics of any sociological enterprise. Concepts mediate between theory and data:

The argument put forward here is that concept-formation in the analysis of sociological data proceeds neither from observation to category, nor from category to observation, but in both directions at once and in interaction ... The process is one in which concepts are formed and modified *both* in the light of empirical evidence *and* in the context of theory. Both theory and evidence can exercise compelling influence on what emerges. (ibid., p. 653)

Out of the present enquiry a number of useful concepts emerge in the manner described by Bulmer. Although they surface from the practices of one small group of workers, the concepts are not restricted to examples of good or bad examples of family therapy but have a wider use in exploring the relationship between worker and client.

The family therapy team, its methods and resources

The family therapy team comprised five qualified social workers and a team leader: three women and three men. Their individual post-qualified experience ranged from two to eight years. Four, including the team leader, were members of an area team. The remaining two were based in a specialist centre dealing with adolescents and their families. The team met as a group on one afternoon a week between 1.00 pm and 5.00 pm in a building conveniently located in the city centre, and not directly associated with the social services department.

The group had existed for about three years. Its origins lay in the common interest of a number of area team workers in the theory and practice of family therapy. The area team as a whole accepted the proposal that this group of workers should offer family therapy as one of the service responses and that suitable families could be referred to the family therapy team through the area's normal allocation channels. Over the three years, the team had evolved and developed its practice of family therapy. Like most family therapists operating in social work settings they blended a number of reasonably compatible family therapy approaches broadly defined as 'brief' and 'systemic', 'structural' and 'strategic' (for example, see Burnham, 1986). 'Hypotheses' were tested, and on some occasions families would be set tasks. The team would normally aim to see a family for a maximum of six sessions. There was no fixed interval between meetings, although the time would normally range between one and three weeks.

The building offered the practitioners three rooms. Theoretically it was possible for the team to see a maximum of four families on any one afternoon but in practice this target was rarely met. A family session would last about an hour. The preferred method of working was to site the therapist in a room with the family. A 'supervisor' would occupy a room next door along with other members of the team if they were not seeing a family at that time. The supervisor watched the proceedings on a television monitor which was connected to a camera and microphone placed in the interviewing room and could also communicate observations and instructions to the therapist during a session using a microphone wired to an 'earbug' worn by the therapist. On their first arrival, the equipment and its purpose would usually be briefly explained to members of the family. Assurances were given about the confidentiality of the material and that all the videotapes would be wiped clean after the completion of treatment.

In advance of the family's visit, the therapeutic team would prepare their thoughts, plan their approach and in some cases propose a 'hypothesis'. The family would arrive and the session run. Throughout the hour the therapist would not only pay attention to the family but would also be listening to the comments of the supervisor. On some occasions, the therapist would take a break and leave the family for five minutes or so to consult with his or her colleagues before returning. At the end of each session, unless it was the family's final meeting, another appointment would be agreed. After each therapeutic encounter, the team would review the session and make notes about such things as content, mood and the system dynamics of the family.

The team itself not only helped members think about and develop their work, it encouraged individuals to keep abreast of new techniques. Social workers attended family therapy workshops and conferences. Consultation was also available. Every month or so, the team was joined by a local consultant psychiatrist who worked in a child guidance clinic and who had a specific interest and expertise in family therapy. He would comment on their practice and give advice on technique and procedure.

The families

During the twelve-month study period, 34 families had been offered family therapy. Eleven families (32 per cent) either declined the offer or failed to keep their first appointment. Ten out of this eleven agreed to be interviewed by me. I was interested in (i) what had brought them to the social services; (ii) what they expected by way of a service or response; and (iii) their reasons for not accepting the offer of family therapy. Twenty-three families (68 per cent) did accept the offer of therapy: 22 of these agreed to be interviewed.

The range of work was typical of the interpersonal problems brought to social services by families with adolescent children. All

Table 3.1   Family structure

	Natural Parents	Adoptive Parents	Natural/ Step-Parent	Single Parent	N=
All referrals:	24% (8)	6% (2)	35% (12)	35% (12)	100% (34)
Families who accepted family therapy:	26% (6)	9% (2)	26% (6)	39% (9)	100% (23)

but one of the cases involved parents experiencing difficulties with one of their children. Generally the parents wanted 'something done about' the child. In the milder cases, they came seeking help and advice. In the more extreme situations, the request was for the removal of the troublesome offspring into local authority care. Material needs were only evident in one family. The remainder appeared to enjoy reasonable economic comfort.

Table 3.1 shows that 70 per cent of the families were either single parent or 'reconstituted'. Of those who accepted family therapy, 65 per cent fell into these two categories. These figures are very similar to those found for the families of children in care or at risk of coming into care (Packman, 1986, Millham *et al.*, 1986, Vernon and Fruin, 1986). Therefore most social work with families in a social services context is in fact work with incomplete or reconstituted families. At the time of referral the age distribution of the 'identified patient' (the difficult child) ranged from 10 to 16 years, with most (77 per cent) falling between 13 and 16 years.

The path to social services
Twelve (35 per cent) of the families had had previous dealings with the social services. They knew that the social services department was an appropriate agency to which to turn when help was needed with a difficult child. The remaining 22 (65 per cent) families were advised to get in touch with a social worker by a variety of other professional workers including general practitioners, health visitors, policemen, teachers and, in one case, a vicar. Mrs Clegg is typical of this group:

> I went to see the doctor who offered me depression pills which is what I don't want, so he got in touch with the social worker and she said try this family therapy.

Mrs Carling was in a state of self-confessed crisis about her twelve-year-old daughter. She had only a vague idea about social services and family therapy:

> All of a sudden I realised I had to do something. I ended up going to the health centre, not knowing what else to do. It was on the door-step. They gave us a cup of tea, they contacted the family therapy branch of the social services. Some very nice lady at the health centre must have wondered what hit her. I rushed up the stairs and she must have thought some sort of mad lady had turned up! I got an appointment through from the social services for something called family therapy. It was completely meaningless!

In a couple of cases families learned of social workers through people who were more familiar with the welfare service. For example, Mr Clark explained that his misbehaving daughter:

> ... went round to see the mother of a friend of hers and this good lady put her up for a fortnight and said that we ... err ... said to us to sort ourselves out and in the meantime we should ... err ... perhaps might need the help of social services.

The experience of family therapy

What did the families make of therapy? Why did some accept the offer for this kind of treatment and others not? The quest here is not to measure the effect of family therapy on specified problem behaviours, though what individual family members got up to after therapy will be mentioned. Instead, the intention is to explore with the families how they perceived, understood and experienced family therapy. The experience of those who receive the efforts of social workers is regarded as an important datum in the evaluation of welfare services. In social work, it is not just a matter of what behaviourally, happens to clients. It is also a case of how they view their involvement with the practitioner. We can either measure the extent of help by examining the future occurrence of the problem condition or we can try to appreciate whether or not people *feel* that they have been helped.

I chose to try to understand the families' experience of receiving therapy. I shall tell their stories and present their views of what they felt and thought had happened in their encounters with social workers. However, the responsibility for the identification of themes and regularities in these experiences lay with me. Although the words are always those of the client, the order in which they are presented and arranged are my creation.

Throughout this exploration of the experience of family therapy there was an interplay between the words of the family members and the thoughts of the researcher – a dynamic relationship, if you like, between data and theory. The understanding of experience is tied to the construction of meaning in the minds of both the researcher and the researched, the reporter and the reported.

With this declaration made, let us now consider the order in which the experiences of family therapy will be presented. The following, which also form the headings for the next three chapters, capture the main concerns of the families:

1. To be engaged
2. To understand
3. To be understood

Within each of these concerns we shall meet a complex, but intriguing mêlée of needs and emotions, hopes and fears, reflections and expectations. These will lead us into the final section in which I shall announce the verdicts on the outcome of family therapy. But, as we shall also see, the idea of a verdict is not such a solid thing as it might first appear. As we move around the concept, it seems to shift, changing its appearance from each new vantage point. This introduces the fundamental question of how we choose to evaluate human affairs.

4 To be engaged

Families seeking help are in a vulnerable and wary state. They have to be approached gently, treated sensitively and won over to what they are about to receive. Coaxing a family into treatment and gaining its confidence is part of the business of 'engaging' the client in the therapeutic enterprise. Family therapists generally advise treading carefully in these very early stages lest the family take flight and are 'lost'. Minuchin and Fishman (1981, pp. 28–9) interpret the phenomenon in systemic terms: although both family and therapist are ostensibly pursuing the same end, the very presence of the therapist upsets the family's homeostasis and this is disturbing. It adds to the discomfort and may lead to the family's withdrawal unless the therapist is alert to what is happening. 'Engagement', according to Masson and O'Byrne (1984, p 28), 'involves careful, thorough self-introduction and a full and repeated explanation of the roles of the worker and the family, of the purpose of the involvement and the manner of proceeding.' This is good advice. Families who are being prepared for therapy are in a taut emotional state and if handled badly will be catapulted out of treatment.

A family with a problem experiences two kinds of anxiety, each of which pulls in the opposite direction. The first is the pain and stress that family members suffer and for which they seek relief and which we might term *problem anxiety*. It draws them *to* therapy. The second is the stress engendered when someone is faced with personal exposure, scrutiny and evaluation. To be examined and possibly judged by others is psychologically threatening. Normally such stress is avoided. It pulls people *away from* therapy. We might call this *service anxiety*. Depending on which is the stronger – the need to relieve pain or the discomfort of examination – a family will either stay in therapy or withdraw.

I have constantly tried to single out one end in human actions which all men unanimously hold as good and which they all seek. I have found only this: The aim of escaping anxiety. Not only have I discovered that all humanity considers this good and desirable, but also . . . no one is moved to act or speak a single word who does not hope by means of this action or word to release anxiety from his spirit. (Ala Ibn Hazm in Kritzeck 1964, p.217)

We can refine the dynamics of this tension a little further. As we have observed, stress causes anxiety and anxiety is something to be reduced. Families experiencing stress can do three things with their anxiety. One, they can employ various psychological manoeuvres (defence mechanisms) to distort the way in which they see the situation. Although the family may not feel the need of outside help, it would not be functioning in a psychologically constructive fashion. Two, the family might try to rid itself of the problem by casting out the member alleged to be the source of stress: 'take this child away'. Three, the family may seek help, not necessarily to have the cause of stress removed but to have him or her treated. But, as we have said, asking the help of others (to remove, advise or treat) invites a judgement which in itself is a potential cause of stress. It is this which we have termed *service anxiety*. A family may handle this second source of stress either by avoidance (withdrawing from therapy) or by attempting to gain some control over the therapeutic encounter so that it is experienced as less arbitrary and one-sided and therefore less stressful. Stress and the anxiety which follows increase dramatically when people do not understand or feel in control of what is happening to them. If events do not make sense and yet seem to be carrying people along they know not where or why, helplessness and panic set in. In the words of one family 'we wanted out'. If people do feel that they understand what is happening and do experience some control over their situation, stress levels fall and they are likely to remain.

Thus, the prospect of help, even when the help itself is a source of anxiety, may be sufficient to keep a family involved. However, if the family does not *perceive* the prospect of any help in the therapeutic enterprise, then this, combined with the stress of exposure, may not outweigh the pain that pushed the family to seek help in the first place: thus, the family withdraws.

So far we have recognized two basic kinds of anxiety:

1. Problem anxiety – which may be high or low – and which, if high, leads to the family seeking help.
2. Service anxiety – which may be high or low – and which, if high, may lead to the family withdrawing from help.

These two, along with the perceived prospect of either being helped or not being helped, generate a range of possible anxiety states which, when balanced against each other, result in a family (i) either remaining or withdrawing from therapy, and (ii) either being or failing to be engaged in the treatment process. It is important to note this distinction between 'remaining' in treatment and 'being engaged' in the treatment process. As we shall see, it is possible to remain in treatment without becoming engaged. Although there are a number of theoretical combinations of these anxiety orientations, the following three were identified in conversation with the 32 families:

1. High problem anxiety + low service anxiety + prospect of being helped = family remains in therapy and becomes engaged.
2. High problem anxiety + high service anxiety + prospect of being helped = family remains in therapy but does not become engaged.
3. High problem anxiety + high service anxiety + no prospect of being helped = family withdraws from therapy and is not engaged.

The level of service anxiety seemed to be affected by three factors: the physical environment including the technical equipment used to facilitate therapy; the method of family therapy itself; and the manner of its delivery. Whether or not the families perceived any prospect of being helped seemed to be influenced by their expectations of the help available, their past experience of social services and their faith, trust and confidence in the proposed method of family therapy. We can now recast these formulations and produce four main 'consumer' categories:

1. Families who remained in therapy, became engaged and held the prospect of help: The Relaxed and Satisfied
2. Families who remained in therapy, but were not engaged yet still held the prospect of help: The Ambivalent
3. Families who withdrew from therapy, were not engaged and did not hold the prospect of help: The Early Leavers
4. Families who were offered therapy but did not accept: The Non-Takers

This classification suggests that all views expressed were consistent within a particular family for the whole therapeutic episode. By and large this was true, but there were exceptions. Occasionally, a husband and wife would offer contrasting experiences of the same event. On the whole, children and young people were least likely to be engaged. The word that any child was most likely to use when asked to comment on his or her experience of family therapy was 'boring'. Moreover, a few families shifted the strength of their views as different aspects of therapy were considered. Whenever possible I shall identify these differences of opinion, although it remains the case that most families were inclined to present a broadly common front.

'The Relaxed and Satisfied'

Only three families who attended therapy said they felt reasonably relaxed and confident from the start. They appreciated the friendly manner of the therapist (who was different in each case). They valued the trouble that he or she took over explaining the procedures. Each family member thought that it was good that they were asked to meet as a family and that it was appropriate to meet away from home. The Vassals, who were keen advocates of family therapy, recalled their first visit:

> *Mrs V:* We told them our problems and they listened to all my problems and Peter's [15 year-old son]. Peter had a look at the TV. He went behind the scenes, didn't you?
>
> *Peter:* Yeh.
>
> *Mr V:* We knew all about the video, you see. They told us before we got started so we felt comfortable with it.
>
> *Mrs V:* They were all very nice. They did it warm and friendly. She called us by our Christian names which relaxes you. . . .
>
> *Mr V:* And we felt better being up at their place which meant that Peter took it serious, didn't you?
>
> *Peter:* Yeh.

Mrs Green also felt it preferable 'going to them. When it's an appointment you make sure you're there, don't you?' And after the experience of her first meeting she went on to recall:

> I wasn't going to go no more until I met the people next door [the supervisors] which I think is fair enough. So next time, she brought them out. We shook hands with them and that was better, like knowing who they all were.

Besides the three families who felt at ease with the method, a couple of others felt the therapist led a double life. Although each family found therapy 'not too bad', they were puzzled about the change which they felt came over the social worker when he or she became a 'therapist'. When not being a therapist, the social worker was said to be a normal, friendly human being. But once in the therapy session the worker changed:

> *Mr Roe:* At our house, before we did the therapy, he was, like, more understanding, nice, you know. . . .
>
> *Mrs Roe:* Yes, and more helpful when he came round to the house than he was at them meetings. At the sessions he was just like a talking dummy.
>
> *Mr Roe:* Well, that's all he was really, wasn't he?

We shall meet these 'talking dummies' again later in this chapter, but whenever most families met a therapist outside therapy they observed that the social worker at large was a much more pleasant creature than the one in therapeutic captivity. Nevertheless, the families which felt comfortable in therapy all agreed that, as Mr Cooper put it, 'bringing us all together as a family was the right idea and they got us all talking which is a thing what we would not have done on our own'.

'The Ambivalent' (and those who felt 'over a barrel')

Asking for help is never easy. Asking for help when you feel a failure as a parent is even more difficult. The need has to be particularly acute for parents to overcome this deep reluctance to put themselves in the hands of the 'welfare'. These were desperate people – at the end of their tether. And yet they remained profoundly ambivalent about approaching the social services. In one and the same act of seeing a social worker there was the promise of relief and the ignominy of failure. 'I felt hostile about having to go,' said Ms Fludd. 'I'm a very independent person normally but for once I just couldn't do it on my own and I suppose I felt a bit of a failure.' For a while at least, these families remained in therapy, hoping that their problems might be resolved. But they did not commit themselves to the process of treatment. Their hearts and minds were not engaged. Apprehension saturated both their experience of the service and their belief in the method. Five families wavered in this fashion. Mrs Downs, a single parent with two children, gives her account:

> My boy beat me up. He's sixteen. He beat me up and smash [*sic*] my home up. Things were really bad. I needed a lot of help. I didn't know what to think or do. I just wanted to see someone 'cos he's been nothing but trouble since I been on my own. . . . I wanted them just to take him away just for a little while to cool him down, but at the social they said try this family therapy thing where you take your children. When they didn't agree to take Dean then, I felt terrible, I felt no one is going to help me. After they told me that I just walked round and round the city for hours. I just didn't want to go home. . . . Well, in the end I did go to see them, I had to really, the whole family. We were in a room with this woman, Susan was her name, with an ear thing and she could hear the others and there was a camera. I felt terrible. I couldn't tell my problems. No way. Not like that. No, you can't. All I wanted was just to get out. Couldn't wait for it to finish. But we went back again. I had to. There was nowhere else. We better keep going, I said, didn't I Dean? It might help but I couldn't see how.

Notes of exasperation also crept into Mrs Bond's reply when I asked her why she had returned a third time to the therapy sessions:

I don't know. I wondered if we carried on with the meetings it might gradually find out something. I still kept saying to them he [her son Wayne] needs to see a psychiatrist, what with all his thieving and violence, but they kept avoiding the question. So I said to you [Wayne], didn't I, 'They don't want to help you. We're wasting our time here'. So I said 'It's up to you Wayne. If you want to go again, you can' and then he said 'I ain't bleeding wasting my time either'. But I turned up for the third one, but Wayne didn't, did you, but that third one was disastrous from the word go.

But if some families remained in therapy in the hope that something helpful might happen, others continued because, in the words of one mother, 'they had us over a barrel'. Or if not over a barrel, then the price to be paid for the prospect of help was to do it the therapist's way or not at all. In a confidential voice, Mrs Downs whispered 'You think they're over you, you see, so even if you are angry you can't say it. Like you've got to answer their question or they'll do something bad.' The Clarks, though, typically could not agree amongst themselves:

> Mrs C: I wasn't very keen on their suggestion of this family therapy. But we thought it might help Karen, didn't we?
> Karen: At first I wanted to go, but. . . .
> Mr C: Yes, I was quite happy to go; for all of us to go. It seemed the best way.
> Mrs C: I felt it was moral blackmail, really, that we all had to go. All the family or nothing was how I felt they put it. That's no real choice.

The Kegg family also felt that they 'had no choice' in both accepting and attending family therapy. We shall dwell on their experience at some length as not only did they have much to tell but their case is used to illustrate the relationship between the 'understandings' of the therapists on the one hand and those of the family on the other. Three perspectives will be woven together: (i) background facts; (ii) the theory and practice of the family therapists in this case; and (iii) the experience and views of the Kegg family. Mrs Kegg in particular remained wary and on her guard throughout the sessions. She said that she was not willing to upset the therapists but neither was she prepared to give them her trust and commitment.

Mrs Kegg had several children by her first relationship before marrying Mr Kegg. He had children by his first marriage but there was no contact. They had no children of their own, but Mr Kegg adopted all of Mrs Kegg's children including her youngest, Emma. When Emma was fifteen, she disclosed to a schoolfriend that she was having a sexual relationship, but not full intercourse, with her adoptive father. Mr Kegg admitted this to the police. Emma was taken into care on a Place of Safety Order and settled with foster parents. Three days later, a case conference suggested that family therapy should be offered to the Keggs. According to the agency's notes, 'The family readily agreed'. The aims of the therapists were 'to strengthen the parental sub-system; encourage Mum and Dad to get Emma to a different school; return Emma home'. Initially six sessions were planned but a seventh was offered and this, too, was completed.

True to their structural leanings, the therapists took as one of their objectives the realignment of generational boundaries: parents should be parents and children should be children and definitely not lovers. The therapists' formulation at the end of the first session read as follows:

> Emma had been allowed to exploit family relationships with control and power inappropriate to her age. Her parents have colluded with this and now this secret is out in the open, Emma has lost that power but with the personal responsibility and guilt the parents feel for what happened, Emma will remain in a position of power.... Mrs Kegg is uncertain whether she is a friend or a mother to Emma.

In her court report the therapist wrote:

> During subsequent family sessions Mr and Mrs Kegg were encouraged and were able to take on a more appropriate parental role. Problems were envisaged, however, as it was felt that Emma would resist reverting to being the child in the family.

The Place of Safety Order was allowed to lapse. At the third session it was agreed that Emma return home, but on two conditions. One, that Emma 'go to school regularly'. And, two, 'the family attend three more family sessions. If they did not fulfil this second condition', the notes continue, 'Emma would be removed from home. They said they would come anyway as they wanted to sort things out.'

However, as predicted, Emma 'resisted'. A couple of months later, and after the fifth session of family therapy, she took an overdose and was admitted to hospital. Although it was felt that there was still a strong element of manipulation on Emma's part, another Place of Safety Order was taken and Emma went to live in a local community home. Whilst there, she was 'observed as being flirtatious, manipulative and making up stories to gain attention and sympathy'. Emma had been in the home two months when Mr Kegg's case came up in court. He was charged with indecent assault and received a conditional discharge.

Two weeks later a vast case conference was held, involving twelve professionals from a variety of disciplines. However, in spite of Emma being described, yet again, as manipulative and Mrs Kegg being regarded by the psychiatrist present as 'really quite screwed up about her relationships with men', Emma was thought not to be at any further risk of sexual abuse. Once more, it was decided to drop care proceedings and allow her home. Another family therapy session was recommended 'to help tidy things up', to sort out feelings about what had happened and about what changes they would like to make in their family, 'but', conclude the conference notes, 'it has got to be they who want it'. The Keggs attended their seventh and final session some eight months after their first. On this last occasion, the therapists found the family cheerful, relaxed, but thoughtful. Everything seemed to be well at home. The notes recorded that 'Mum and Dad's sexual relationship was O.K.'. The therapists and the family reviewed the sessions. It was agreed, amongst other things, that the therapy had helped the Keggs through the shock of what happened, it had helped Mr Kegg take responsibility for what had happened and it had encouraged both mother and father to be more parental towards Emma.

How did the Keggs view all this? What did they feel about family therapy? Looking back on their experience, Mr and Mrs Kegg saw themselves playing a different game. They wanted Emma back home. However, they also knew that in order for this to happen it had to be on whatever terms were laid down by social services. This happened to be a course of family therapy which they duly accepted. The only thing they felt they had some control over was the content of their replies. We shall follow their views and trace their moves as they reflect on being 'over a barrel', on being careful, on the therapeutic techniques and on the overall experience.

On being 'over a barrel'

Mr K: You see, there was a committee of about six sitting in the other room watching us on a television which I didn't like at all. . . .

Mrs K: It was awful, but what could we do?

Mr K: They said they didn't want to be known in case we saw them in the city or anywhere.

Mrs K: But we had to be known, didn't we. Like when I'm walking down the street and someone perhaps look at you and you think 'was that one of them?' you know, that's awful. If they was trying to help us why couldn't they have sat down like normal civilized people or come round to our house and had a cup of tea. I'd have preferred it that way. It would have been more friendly. You could have seen who you were talking to instead of those video things.

Mr K: We felt like guinea pigs.

Mrs K: But you see we didn't have no choice but to go, did we, really. They set the terms.

Mr K: We never knew them, never knew their names or nothing.

Mrs K: Why couldn't they say things to our face? Perhaps they've never had children, how do I know. How do I know if they're all men or all women? I don't know. But as I said, we couldn't say no to anything because I don't think any of us would have had a chance of being together now.

On being careful

Mrs K: Half the answers we gave, we didn't exactly lie, but we were conscious ... er ... we watched what we say; you were extra careful because they could run them videos back every time to check on what you had said so you were extra careful.

Mr K: You were frightened to say the wrong things.

Mrs K: You thought to yourself 'Now what do they want us to say here? Like they told me I was a very deep person. I'm not! I'm just very careful, very careful what I say.

Mr K: Really it meant that partly it was all a waste of time because all you said is what you thought they wanted you to say.

On the therapeutic techniques

Mrs K: Like one week they said 'why do all the men sit together on one side and all the girls on the other?' and they made us change. I thought it was weird. I mean, it don't make any difference where you sit, really. All them meetings, well, they weren't normal, if you see what I mean.

Mr K: And then they said we weren't being a mother and a father, we were too much like friends, which is silly. They said you got to make more rules and regulations in the house. Lay down the law like what a father would do.

Mrs K: And we've got to go out on our own and not with the family which is what we normally do and have a good time at the club. I thought that was weird. We took no notice.... And then there was one session when they went on about our sex lives, and we said it was all right. It was rude really.

Mr K: We had a row about that afterwards, didn't we?

Mrs K: Yeh, I said I wasn't going to come no more.

Mr K: And I said we had no choice.

Mrs K: They always bring sex into it and I can't see what sex has got to do with it. You don't want to talk about certain things with the children there. It's wrong.

Mr K: I felt more comfortable when the children weren't there. More relaxed. You see, Robert, our son, he's backward, like, and they insisted we bring him. Now Robert, being backward, you know, you could give him a thousand pound and say to him 'Now don't tell no-one'. But he would. Well because our problem was very personal and we didn't want one to know about it, bringing Robert, which we were told we had to, put me on edge which wasn't right.

On the overall experience

Mr K: Well, I think some good did come out of it. You see the state my wife was in, I don't think ... er ... personally myself, I don't think we would have sorted it out to start with on our own and we'd have a complete bust up. She'd have gone her way and I'd have gone mine, because, well, I think it did help, like, keep us together, you know, to help us get through the crucial part of the first two or three weeks, maybe not necessary [*sic*] later, I agree, but those first few weeks when. . . .

Mrs K: No, I disagree. I know my mind. I might be the nervy type and highly strung. At some times I felt it made matters worse, like when they told us to start treating Emma like a mother and father should, it made it worse.

Mr K: True, she went completely the opposite bloody way so we went back to our usual way.

Mrs K: You see, I've never agreed with a stranger sorting out your problems. I'd rather have, well, done what I've always done, stand on my own two feet and when I need help go to my doctor who does help me a lot.

The Keggs, then, came to the sessions whenever asked. They remained *in* therapy but, particularly in Mrs Kegg's case, they sought not to be a committed part *of* therapy. Along with several other families they did stay the course but were not engaged. Similarly, the families that we meet next were not engaged, but they left well before the end of treatment, with most calling it a day after two or three sessions.

'The Early Leavers'
On the face of it, families in this category had problems every bit as stressful as others met in the study population. True, like all but one of the families, they saw themselves as voluntary clients and so felt free to leave therapy at any time, but their anxieties about asking for and receiving help did not diminish. In fact, more often than not they increased as they experienced the techniques and technology of the family therapy team. In particular, three things appeared to maintain or heighten anxiety: the *machines*; the *method*; and the *manner*. Their effect was to frustrate engagement without which therapy was doomed to failure.

The technical equipment, the treatment method and the style of the therapist were each experienced as a potential barrier. Together they placed a great distance between the therapists and the families. They denied the situation any warmth. With stress already running high and the prospect of help receding fast, these families chose not to stay in therapy. Altogether, just over half of the families who accepted therapy fell into this category.

The machines

If it is stressful to expose weakness and failure to one other person, such stress is magnified many fold if that weakness and failure are to be witnessed by several people, who remain unknown and who tape all that you do and say on a video recorder. These families found their levels of anxiety soaring when faced with the technical equipment. They could not concentrate on what was happening and wanted to 'escape' as soon as possible. Instead of surroundings which were physically and psychologically soft and in which bruised, fragile minds could open up, the families found themselves in a hard, probing, aggressive environment. They felt vulnerable and under threat. Their only defence was to ward off the intrusion.

Although a few of the children were curious about the camera and 'wanted to be on television', most, like Sharon (aged twelve) found it 'silly' and 'embarrassing'. Trixie (aged eleven) said: 'I got all wound up before the second meeting and I was sick 'cos I didn't want to go with them cameras and things.' Some felt caged. They were ready to 'explode'. Tracey Needham (aged fourteen), interviewed in a children's home, remembered:

> I got really fed up with people looking at me, I felt trapped, you know, and more angrier. I wanted to get out and answer all their questions quickly and just get out. They kept pushing into our lives. They were just driving me nuts and I just wanted to get away and not go no more. I felt like chucking things around 'cos I just couldn't stand it.

Although the camera was a small portable unit on a lightweight tripod it loomed much larger in the sights of some families. Mrs Skiddles smiled as she recollected:

> It might have been ten foot square, that camera, it was so apparent to me. Well, if I'd have had my way I would have been out of that door and down those stairs and out! Big Brother's watching! I wondered what I'd let myself in for.

Emotions clearly affect perception. 'The camera was the biggest thing in the room,' echoed Mrs Spree. 'There was nothing else there, nothing comfortable. I personally felt ... uhmm ... we thought, you know, *family* therapy, like, it would be cosy.'

It was the therapists' policy and practice to explain the presence of the machines beforehand, but many families felt ill-prepared for the experience. For some, it was only a short step from discomfort to panic. The set-up was calculated to produce, in the words of one parent, 'feelings of paranoia'. Mrs Pound said that the presence of the camera inhibited her normally very boisterous boys who became 'dead quiet and didn't act at all natural'. She, too, felt 'ill at ease'. Mrs Needham said she was petrified: 'I had nightmares about them cameras, really. Dreaming about them for days afterwards, I was.' Later in the interview she and her elder daughter returned to the theme:

Mrs N: The television was there to help them interrogate you; that's the only word what I can use. They ask you questions and you try to answer them the best way you think.

Kate: I felt they was spying on us.

Mrs N: You see, what they used it for was, like, if she [the therapist] wasn't asking the right sort of questions, they [the supervisors] would correct her and whisper in her ear through the microphone and get her to keep on at us.

Mr and Mrs Street were also upset by their experience, but were strong enough to object to the machinery being used. Their marriage was rocky and there was growing violence between father and the second eldest son. The police had been involved and it was they who recommended social services, who in turn advised a course of family therapy. Mrs Street recalls their first and only visit:

We went with an open mind. We were shown into a room and left for a while – I imagine purposefully – I may be wrong. In that room was a camera and a microphone and I shook my head at Keith [her husband] and we never spoke to each other because we were obviously upset in case they were listening to us and then when the young lady came in she said, 'would we mind if my colleagues in another room could watch and listen to what you're saying', I was horrified. I said 'No way! If your colleagues want to come into this room and be with us, fair enough, but no way am I going to be filmed.' It may help them, but quite frankly it turned me off and if they were to use it I was about to walk out and leave. It made me very upset and angry and really at that stage I didn't want to know. Quite frankly it took me a long while to answer her questions because I was so uptight about the whole affair.

The method

Again, the families in this category wanted to feel reassured and relaxed before they were prepared to lay themselves before the therapist. However the mechanics of therapy failed to reassure and settle the parents of these families. Three aspects in particular kept them on edge: being away from home; the use of unseen and unheard supervisors; and the presence of their own children when discussions turned to adult relationships.

For nearly all families *home* seemed the right place to consider family matters. In their natural environment the families felt they would behave naturally. The therapists would not only find them at ease but would gain a more accurate picture of how they got on together. 'I'd rather they had come here to see us,' said Mrs Ruff. 'I'd certainly have been more relaxed.' Mr Rivers didn't like 'mass meetings' at all, while Mrs Sloope felt 'You can say things in your own home where at their place you keep thinking "should I say that here?"' 'Much better'; declared Mrs Skiddles, 'to sit in your own home, have a talk, have a fag and a cup of tea and you can relax and when you're relaxed you can talk, natural like, and not try to be perfect as you do there.'

However it was the *supervisors* – unseen, unheard – that caused most disquiet. Families fantasized about them. The more tense the family, the more Kafkaesque was their experience. Away from their home, placed in a small room at the top of an old building with the sounds of the city but a distant murmur, confronted by a camera pointing directly at them, the families felt removed from the familiar routines of everyday life. Some said it was like being at a secret trial. 'You see, with all them back there it all went on behind your back.' The seemingly bizarre techniques used by the therapists were seen as just another way of 'investigating the case'. Mr Spree was the stepfather of fourteen year-old Rachel, but it was Mrs Spree who was most upset about her daughter's difficult behaviour. They recounted their first session:

> *Mr S:* Well first, what I felt like was that it was them against us, There was no relationship at all. The panel in the next room could feedback to the person in the room with us, but we had nothing directly to do with them. They were like 'Big Brother' out there. I found it very disconcerting.
>
> *Mrs S:* We didn't even know who was in there.
>
> *Mr S:* It could have been anyone.
>
> *Mrs S:* I mean, if they'd given us a cup of tea first, that would have been helpful.
>
> *Mr S:* The panel kept interrupting. It was very off-putting, very confusing. We never seemed to get anywhere.

Mrs S: He'd say something like . . . er . . . after he got a message from the panel, 'Oh, I've got to bring in Rachel now' and you were cut short. I felt like a guinea pig.

Mr S: I did, actually, too. We were like puppets and it was like they were experimenting with us, because they'd found this new thing, this camera and things, and could try out certain techniques of interviewing.

Mrs Ruff, who felt 'on trial' and found it all 'weird' said, 'They kept going out, then came back and asked some more questions. They said they needed to get to the root of the problem.' And like a number of parents, Mrs Ruff believed that being on trial clearly meant that she was being accused of failing to be a good parent. She was to blame for the family's troubles. But at least Mrs Ruff felt she knew of what she was being accused. Mrs Kay did not even know that!

Mrs K: They looked at you funny. They seemed more interested in my past than Darren's. I felt that I was the one in the wrong, like it was me on trial, you know, like they were saying 'you're the guilty party'.

D H: Guilty of what?

Mrs K: Ah, that's it you see! I don't know. You never know!

However, if it was a trial, then Mr Rivers felt that it was not a just one for 'if you are in court, you can see the judge, you can see the jury. You can even pick the jury! But not there.' Thus, if the supervisors had to exist, the universal preference was at least to meet them, 'shake hands and say hello', and in many cases have them in the same room 'instead of hiding themselves away where for all I know they could be laughing theirselves stupid at us and what we was saying'.

The presence of *children*, particularly the alleged malefactor's brothers and sisters who were thought both innocent and irrelevant to the issue, was not thought conducive to open, easy or appropriate conversation. This was especially so when discussion focused on the relationship between parents. Mrs Spree said:

If we ever did go back again it would have to be on our own, not with the children. I don't want to drag my kids through it. I mean, I don't think children benefit from seeing their parents completely crumble in front of them.

The Streets were happy to have their difficult sixteen year-old son along, but not their three other children. But Mr and Mrs Rivers wanted their needs attended to and this certainly did not concern any of their children as they saw it:

> Mr R: This family meeting thing is all wrong to my way of thinking. It was Linda [his wife] and me what needed the help.
> Mrs R: You can't sit there in front of your kids, can you?
> Mr R: I can't sit in front of my children and say [pointing to his wife] 'You done this or that, you bag' now, can I? My kids will be thinking 'whatever is going on here?' Now I'll tell you why I think they want the kids there. A kid will never lie, will he, so you can sit there and say what you like but I felt them children were there to draw information out. What I wouldn't tell them, the kids would and that is all wrong to my way of thinking.

The manner

If the room felt uncomfortable, the camera intrusive and the supervisors inquisitorial, any remaining hopes of reducing stress lay with the therapist. His or her personal style and manner was taken as a critical indicator as to whether or not this was likely to happen. Family members were extra alert to the mood and personality of the therapist. Of course, as we have heard already, some families thought the therapist herself was just as much a victim as the family under scrutiny. All the power was believed to lie with the supervisors who, though unseen themselves, were all-seeing. The therapist was under their control and bidding. So even when the therapist was perceived as a 'nice guy', in the context of therapy he or she was perceived as bowing to the will of the supervisors. They were the 'boss' and, so far as some families were concerned, probably 'the bosses of the department too'. The friendliness of the therapist, if it was present at all, could only be seen outside of therapy.

> Mr Pye: He [the therapist] was the middle-man, you see. They fed the questions through him. He was all right on his own, a very nice person in fact. Like, when he came round ours and he was very nice.
> Mrs Pye: He even agreed with us on a lot of things.
> Mr Pye: Well, in fact he agreed with us three different things which them at the back in their meeting, like, they didn't agree.
> Mrs Pye: But of course, he didn't have a leg to stand on.
> Mr Pye: His hands were tied, you see. But, personally, you know, him hiself, he seemed very nice. A very reasonable person.
> Mrs Pye: Very nice. There's good and there's bad but he was one of the good ones. He listened whereas the others thought it was a family problem. So, you see, when he [as the therapist] was seeing us at this family therapy he couldn't be his self.

The trouble was, though, that for many families, the social worker took on a 'therapeutic persona' which depersonalized him or her. The technique seemed to take over his or her normal manner. The social worker became less friendly, less approachable and more an instrument of the supervisors to whom literally they were wired. Or, if not an instrument of the supervisors, then they were described as 'sergeant majors', 'sharp' or 'false', at least in the eyes of the most stressed families. As with the Pyes, Mrs Needham found her therapist 'friendly when she was round ours', but unaccountably 'quite stroppy at the meetings, like she wanted you to answer properly what she'd asked. We got to the stage when we got to the door and say to each other "should we bother to go in?" and when we did we went in full of smiles hoping that we wouldn't get questioned so much.' The Sprees did not find it so aggressive. Rather, their imagery harked back to the 1970s:

Mrs S: The only people we saw in that building were slightly alternative, like ageing hippies, weren't they?
Mr S: That's right. I couldn't relate.
Mrs S: He was probably into CND and Save the Whale. He looked a bit ecological.
Mr S: He wasn't the sort of person that you felt you could build a relationship with.
Mrs S: It seemed really as if he was just playing a game, you know.

The non-takers

In the study year, eleven families were offered family therapy but either they did not accept or failed to turn up for their first appointment. There was no alternative service available. I visited ten of these families hoping to understand why, having gone so far as to contact social services, they decided not to take advantage of the service offered. Three main reasons were given: a past experience of social workers and their methods; the lack of confidence in the type of help proposed (family therapy); and the manner in which they felt they were received by social workers when they first asked for help. Some families gave more than one of these reasons. However, all the families gave the impression that they were looking for something, although they were not always clear what. In interview, their reflections conveyed an air of disappointment, sadness or occasionally anger. If they were not looking for some quiet sympathetic understanding, then they were looking for immediate action: 'take my boy away now' or 'come and see my daughter and tell her to mend her ways or else she will be in care'. However, they felt the response seemed evasive and insensitive; the attitude was perceived as one of 'take it or leave it'. 'She was very abrupt', remembered Mrs Ives, 'and asked us lots of funny questions, so when she said have this family therapy I thought "no thank you".' Mr Hogg felt the social worker at the duty office 'sounded totally disinterested as if I was a pain in the arse. You need something like the Samaritans, not bloody social workers. I mean if you get a toothache you don't, you can't, wait a week for some airy-fairy thing, can you now, be honest'.

In fact, most families, whether or not they accepted therapy, had expectations of what sort of help would be appropriate although it rarely coincided with the actual service offered. But whereas the 'takers' were prepared at least to try the unexpected suggestion of family therapy, the 'non-takers' were not. They were not offered the kind of help they felt would be of use or appropriate to their needs. With a sigh and sometimes a curse, they declined the offer of being treated as a family.

Moreover, if the family had experienced social work help in the past and that experience was judged to be poor, any feeling that the latest offer of help was likely to repeat the earlier experience resulted in rejection of the service offered. Mrs Block said that she had had earlier dealings with social workers over her daughter: 'What these social workers say is all right in theory,' she reflected, 'but no bloody use in practice. All this family stuff sounds clever, but they made a right balls-up before with my family so there was no way I was having that again.' Mr and Mrs Flaggon had:

> . . . a big, burly sixteen year-old. He's always been difficult and his school, which is for the maladjusted, knows all about it. He breaks things, he's violent around the house and he steals. He's put a great strain on our marriage. We don't want him to go away, but, well, we just wanted a bit of support, an odd break and, you know, somewhere you can ring when you're absolutely desperate. And we were desperate, you know. No one seemed to really understand. We had this family meeting thing before and my husband wouldn't have nothing more to do with it. I just wanted someone to come round and see me, then, to talk to and maybe give us some advice. I was on the 'phone for an hour and a half and I thought they understood. And then the next day this letter comes saying there is an appointment for this family therapy. I was so upset and angry. As far as I'm concerned there is no social services. We never went.

Mrs Nails was new to social services. She spent two hours at the duty office asking for a visit that evening but was advised that family therapy would be more appropriate. 'I came away feeling very despondent', she said, 'like a pricked balloon.' She did not keep her appointment.

Engaging advice

Although a few families remained implacably hostile to family therapy, a large number, including some of the early leavers, sensed that 'there was something in it'. But the assault the technique made on their everyday assumptions about how to conduct a social encounter with a professional worker was, in most cases, too much. They either failed to engage or simply left. The method of family therapy departed significantly from (i) what they had expected; (ii) their usual experience of relating to an outside agent; and (iii) their usual experience of relating to one another within the family. If social workers are to take families into territory which is unexpected, unfamiliar and unnerving, advance preparations and detailed briefings are required. People will not follow, they will not become engaged in emotional expeditions without discussion, without rehearsal and without reassurance. 'Something like that', said Mrs Fludd, 'has to be done really slowly with me. I mean, I could see what they were trying to get at, but I couldn't keep my mind on what they were doing because it was all so odd, you know.'

Families wanted to be told about the procedure. They wanted to understand the need for the camera and the supervisors. Introductions to the personnel and the equipment were felt to be very important. They would have welcomed explanations about the proposed method of help so that they could reorientate themselves to what, after all, is a most unusual way of behaving in most people's experience. 'Talking like that,' said Mrs Skiddles, 'in that way, asking funny questions, which were interesting, don't get me wrong, but it wasn't our way, if you see what I mean, and it, like, well, we didn't know what to say.'

Perhaps the obvious comparison is with a medical procedure. Good practice requires the surgeon or physician to take the patient through the proposed procedure, to answer questions, to detect worries and seek to give reassurance where it is appropriate. All families felt that this introductory phase was critical. It represented a transition from 'everyday ways of behaving' to an 'extraordinary way of behaving' to which they were not necessarily opposed, but which did require some psychological preparation without which engagement would not take place. 'Relax me' was the prevailing message. Families wanted to be approached gently and sensitively, thoughtfully and slowly. What is a familiar routine and taken-for-granted way of operating for the therapist is a unique and peculiar experience for the family. The therapist must never forget this. 'Now if he had sat us down, had a cup of tea with us first,' suggested Mrs Sloope, 'and told us about what this was all about and given us a bit of a breather and a chance to get the feel of things, then I might have felt less terrified and then I might have come back.'

5 To understand

Families who undertook therapy wanted to understand two things: their problem and their experience of family therapy. People like to feel in control of events and experiences, otherwise they do not know what is happening or what might happen next. Not to be in control or to know what is happening is disconcerting and, generally, this is to be avoided. The first step in achieving control is to try and *make sense* of what is taking place. If it is less puzzling, then it is less threatening; if it is more predictable, then it is more manageable. The sense that is made of a difficult experience may not necessarily be a very useful or appropriate one. Nevertheless, people do seek to impose meaning on their experiences. They interpret situations.

Going to visit a social worker was one strategy used by families hoping to make sense of their difficulties. The other person might provide an explanation of what was happening. Certainly, the social workers as therapists did have ideas of what was going on in the families which they saw. During the sessions, the balance of power lay with the therapeutic team because the prevailing definition of the situation was structured in their terms. Families had three options: they could see the situation in the same terms and accept it; recognize the therapists' definition but reject it; or fail to understand the therapists' definition and remain confused. If the 'explanation' itself became a puzzle, the family were then faced with two uncertainties of which to make sense.

Of course, so far as the social workers themselves were concerned, their explanation was implicit in the method of treatment. Rather than hold an intellectual discussion about the way families function and members communicate, the therapists sought change through action. In this they might be compared to behaviourists. Instead of helping families change their meaning in order to alter experience, families are encouraged to change their experience in order to alter meaning. By provoking new experiences and unaccustomed ways of behaving and communicating, families can be helped to reconceive their relationships with one another. The conventional therapeutic order is reversed. Instead of 'understanding leads to behavioural change', family therapists go for 'behavioural change leads to understanding'. But if the family fails to change its behaviour, for whatever reasons, then, by definition, it will not learn to understand or explain its own behaviour in the terms implied in systemic family therapy. The family is still left with a need to make sense of its problem, on top of which it has now to account for the experience of therapy itself.

Families who were not clear about what was happening attempted to make sense of their experience within their more customary frames of reference. Their seemingly 'odd' experience with the therapists was explained in terms of what the family thought a group of social workers might 'really' be doing. Their speculations about what was really going on included the idea that the workers were conducting a new technique of investigation, that they were the subjects of an 'experiment' with problem families and that it was a way of avoiding giving practical help and advice.

For any one family, understandings and explanations arose with respect to both their problem and their experience of therapy. These understandings and explanations were constructed either in sympathy with those of the family therapists, or in opposition. Two positions were identified;

1. Understandings between families and therapists which converged.
2. Understandings between families and therapists which diverged.

Convergent understandings

The understanding of therapy reached by these families was not, of course, couched in the same language as that used by the therapists. Nevertheless, each family understood that the therapists were helping them explore what was happening amongst themselves. In particular, it was recognized that members were being helped to say what could not be said or was not being said. This allowed individuals to learn the views and feelings of other members of the family. In turn, this helped alter attitudes and behaviours and so improve mutual understandings. Simply having the opportunity to talk was recognized as an important event. In Mrs Cooper's words:

> It meant we had to get together which was an achievement in itself, and if we were together we could talk and I said if you can talk about it you're at least half way to getting there . . . It sort of got you to see things different which is what we needed.

In understanding what was happening in therapy, a family came to understand itself and the nature of its problem. This is how Mrs Green saw one exercise:

Well, Jason, I shocked him with some of the things I came out with.
He couldn't just believe it. He hadn't no idea how I saw him and
felt about him. It did him good to hear. All of us really. We said
things we couldn't have said at home on our own. Like, they gave
us a piece of paper each and, like, said 'how did I want to see Jason
to be more of a son than a man' or something. Jason was given one
'how could he be a better son to his mother' and that. Louise got one
as well.

The Vassals had been upset by their son's behaviour. 'He lies and
steals. He's out of hand. He causes arguments between us.' Of
family therapy, Mrs Vassal said that 'other people sitting there
helping you with your problems is what makes it don't seem so
much of a burden to you.' Her husband added, 'You need an
outsider to keep us having a quiet discussion instead of a bawling
match. Everyone had to say what they think, which was good.' It
appeared to the therapist that Mr and Mrs Vassal were not acting
together as a parental team and that their incoherent reaction to
Peter's misbehaviour simply perpetuated this division. The aim
was 'to disengage Peter's behaviour from the marital disharmony'.
Mr and Mrs Vassal were encouraged 'to keep on parenting together'
and 'to go out together' and together treat Peter as the child. 'The
idea was to get us working together,' said Mr Vassal, 'which was
good. We go out now whereas before we didn't and we don't argue
no more about what to do when Peter plays up, which he don't so
much anyway.'

Karen Clark was growing more difficult, staying out late at
night, drinking 'with a rough crowd'. She wanted to leave home.
Mr Clark's health was not very good. The therapeutic team saw
an 'Atlantic Ocean' between Mr and Mrs Clark. There was felt
to be very little communication in the family. The records note
that 'Maybe Karen by leaving home was saying "I can cope,
don't worry about me, look after Dad"'. In the first session, it
was felt that 'mother nags and interrupts; Karen withdraws; Dad
is very verbose, rambles and interrupts and yet is not very good
at expressing his feelings'. Mum and Dad gave Karen 'mixed
messages'. The therapeutic strategy was to help Mr and Mrs
Clark talk and work together and give Karen a coherent
response:

> *Mr C:*   We have a lot of talk but no real conversation. Nobody tries
> to explain themselves or tries to understand the other side.
> So, really, it was about the family having to pull itself
> together, with him [the therapist] being a catalyst, and us
> using our conversation to be able to build up our
> relationships.

Mrs C: I could see that, yes, but they did go up some blind alleys and miss the point, I thought.

Mr C: I don't think they were missing the point. It is of course different for me. I go to meetings all the time at work. All meetings are of course different. You keep silent for a time then interject a point of view which is possibly totally different from what somebody has said. Therefore I have a different view of these things.

Divergent understandings

There was a category of families who did recognize the basis on which the therapists were understanding family affairs, but the experts' explanation was rejected. Here is one view of a family sculpt:

> Half way through a session we all had to get up, stand in a circle and each one had to place the other next to ... er ... in importance in the family, like Mum and Dad, like who would you place near them, you know, which was, like playing games. It was supposed to get us to see how each one of us saw everyone else but it never really got us seeing us how we really are. I thought it was very silly.

The Peckers were not impressed with the ideas that the boundaries between the generations was lost. Mrs Pecker:

> I suppose it was something to do with how relationships and all that were and how we got on in different ways in the family. The social worker thought that Kate [her daughter] and me was more like sisters 'cos we can talk to each other about anything. But we didn't reckon much to their way, the way they thought our family was because we know how our family works but they seemed to have turned it round, you know.

The remaining families in this group thought that therapy was a 'weird' or 'peculiar' experience. It was so outside their normal experience they could find no obvious way in which they could make sense of what had happened. The way they were asked to respond and behave did not lead to a new experience. They remained locked in their established habits. Therapy could only be viewed 'as a very funny way of going about things', although they naturally assumed that the therapists 'must have been up to something'. Some families devised explanations. Others left therapy 'completely bewildered' and 'could make head nor tail of it'.

In families whose understanding diverged from that of the

therapists, the most common view was that the technique represented some elaborate but obtuse way of furthering investigations into their case. Mrs Spree decided that 'They were investigating, I suppose. Obviously following some procedure according to some book, otherwise I couldn't see what they were trying to do.' But Mrs Ruff was in no doubt about what 'they were really doing'.

> At the second meeting they told us they couldn't get anything they wanted out of the first. They asked all about my past, what life was like with the husband, how the children were when they were younger, I thought 'nosey lot of sods! Prying into my private life when they should be trying to help Sean instead of trying to see where I was at fault.'

A couple of families, who had been expecting advice, continued to think that they were receiving it, albeit in a roundabout way. But they 'didn't reckon much to what they suggested'. The advice was thought to be poor. The therapists on their part were not seeking to give direct advice but were attempting to help families restructure relationships and break established patterns of communication which were maintaining the problem. There were occasions when the therapists did make direct suggestions. However, the intention was that the family would find it difficult or inappropriate to carry it out which would have the effect of producing behaviour which the therapists thought to be more appropriate. These 'paradoxical injunctions' by their very nature could not be explained to a family in advance. For example Mrs Bond was thought to be too involved with her son Wayne. He represented the loving, companionable side of how a husband ought to be, which led to 'enmeshment' between mother and son. The therapists wished to break this and, paradoxically, advised that 'Mother and Wayne spend *much more* time together' in the hope that Mrs Bond and Wayne would react against such advice and separate. Although Mrs Bond did not understand the thinking behind the suggestion, nevertheless, from the point of view of the therapists, the technique worked. Mrs Bond recalled:

> They said I should take Wayne out to the pictures, take him to the pub, anywhere I go, but it was silly, because Wayne has got his own way of life and his views. He's sixteen and his ways are different to mine. So we didn't bother, did we. I mean you can't expect a sixteen year-old boy to go to the pictures with his Mum, can you?'

However, about half the families felt 'bewildered'. They did not know what the family therapists were hoping to achieve, and understood even less about the methods used. Many families could not understand the need to have the whole family present – particularly those children who were not seen as a problem. The more generous comments credited the therapists with knowing what was going on, even if the family did not: 'I suppose they knew what they were doing but to tell you the truth I hadn't a clue. It was all very strange but I suppose there must have been a reason but I never found it out.' Mrs Needham and her daughters could not understand why the social workers kept asking everyone for their point of view:

Mrs N: I wanted to know how *I* could cope with Tracey's problems. What was the best way but they never did give me help on how to cope with her. We just sat and talked and I couldn't see the point.

Tina: It was irrelevant questions, like, for example, there was one question, like, 'would you like to jump into bed with your step-dad?' and I couldn't see why they asked such a question nor see what that had got to do with my sister. It was stupid and I didn't like that at all. So I didn't go again.

Mrs N: To my way of thinking they seemed more interested in every other member of the family apart from Tracey, which was . . . er . . . you know, didn't make no sense to me at all.

The most puzzling requirement for most families who did not understand the nature of the method was the need to have children other than the 'problem child' present. 'My boys kept asking me why they had to go "'cos it's Andrew's problem not ours"', said Mrs Pound. 'They kept saying the problem was through the whole family but they seemed to bypass Andrew all the time which got us nowhere.' Mrs Rivers thought:

To hell with you. There's nothing wrong with the rest of our family. It's not a family problem. It's Danny's problem and it's no good trying to tell me different. The girls went under protest. Said it was unfair because they'd done nothing. I felt that we were all being blamed for Danny's problems.

George Sloope, aged fifteen, was causing his mother considerable distress. He stole, played truant and lied. George was part of a large family. The therapists felt that Mrs Sloope and most of her children were deeply enmeshed, while Mr Sloope was 'disengaged' from the family. Mrs Sloope was overweight and prone to feeling unwell. The aim was 'To disengage the children from looking after Mum inappropriately'. But the Sloopes never got the hang of what was happening and left after one session:

Mrs S: They never kept to one subject. They kept asking questions to everybody and going from one to another.

George: They kept on about schools, family, education and things.

Mrs S: She said, 'Do you and your husband get on well together? Do the children and your husband get on?' I thought 'Well, what's that got to do with George's problem of shoplifting?'

Vicky: They wanted to know if me and my sister got on which don't circle George [sic].

Mrs S: I just didn't understand the questions. I mean I understood them but I didn't understand why they'd been asked. It went on for an hour.

George: An hour and eleven minutes. I measured it.

Mrs S: He's got one of them watches. God knows where from.

Vicky: I couldn't see why they kept going on about my personal things, you know to do with me and it wasn't me what was the problem.

Mrs S: It didn't seem fair on Vicky. I felt very low at the end of it. Delapidated, I think. I felt sorry for Vicky. They'd done nothing for him [George] who was the problem.

Making sense of behaviour and behaviour for making sense

The manner in which understanding is gained is curiously different for the therapists on the one hand and the families on the other. In systemic terms, although the families could only make better sense of their situation by behaving differently, this was not so for the therapists. Their ability to make sense of what was happening was theoretically derived, informed by intellectual effort and not behavioural experience. In other words, whereas the therapists could learn new meanings which would produce new experiences, this formula was not extended to the families who were required to expose themselves to new experiences in order to gain new meanings. For the therapists, knowledge produced their practice, while, for the families, practice was expected to produce knowledge. Thus, therapy which failed to produce behavioural changes did not lead to a family's better understanding of either its problem or its experience of therapy. It was left trying to make sense of family therapy in moral and political terms rather than those of General Systems Theory. Hence, at least for families who did not understand, their explanation was that probably they were being investigated and judged, manipulated and used, misled and maligned by a technique that otherwise defied understanding.

6   To be understood

For most people, there is a need to be understood. The feeling that someone else can sense and understand matters as we experience them consoles as well as affirms our condition. This need is particularly acute when things are not going well, when pain and despair lower the spirit. It is at this point that we need to introduce a conceptual distinction between two acts: explanation and understanding. We are back with the social worker as scientist and the social worker as helper, or as Hugh England (1986) prefers (and I am inclined to follow), the social worker as artist.

Explaining someone or something, in England's sense, is a scientific act. The concepts and measures that are used to explain the phenomenon come from outside the phenomenon itself. In our case, families are taken to be functioning objects or systems capable of objective description and explanation. Hypotheses are made about possible modes of operation. Essentially, the therapist relates to the family as subject to object. The family is to be explained in his or her terms. The therapist seeks to correct aspects of the system that he or she determines to be at fault. Once mended, the family can resume effective functioning.

Understanding someone (and it must be the individual for there is no subjective entity beyond the person in this outlook) is a humanistic act. Understanding another's experience can only come from seeing things from his or her point of view. The social worker as artist relates to the other person as subject to subject. England maintains that 'The task of the social worker is always to understand the meaning of experience and to communicate that understanding' (1986, p. 25). He develops a persuasive thesis that the social worker, like the artist, seeks to understand the meaning of experience and for that meaning to be communicated in order that the experience might be understood. England quotes the argument of Raymond Williams that, for each one of us, it is a matter of personal importance to 'describe' our experience. In communicating this description we create ourselves and develop an understanding of who we are and what is happening. People must give meaning to events in order to make sense of them for without sense or meaning the world becomes a very disturbing, threatening place. England continues:

Williams's account shows that people *make* their understanding of the world, that description through communication is an essential part of understanding, and that communication must be exact, and effectively shared. In the most fundamental way, each person's ability to make sense, and to organize an understanding of the world, depends upon the ability to communicate about that understanding. 'Reality' is only maintained by its communication, and such communication is particularly urgent at times of stress ... Williams's account ... gives an added clarity to that process of the recognition of experience which is of such profound importance. It makes fundamental sense of the relief and gratitude people show in response to accurate understanding, for they have, literally, been helped to exist. (England, 1986, p. 112)

The social worker as scientist does not attempt to understand the meaning which the other gives to his experience. She wishes simply to explain behaviour with a mind to 'fixing' whatever it is that is at fault. The client is passive. His behaviour occurs as evidence which helps the expert refine her explanation. But, if to understand and to be understood are basic characteristics of being human, as the humanists believe, then we might expect this to emerge in the accounts given by clients of their experience of family therapy. To what extent did they wish to be understood? Did they feel that they *were* understood?

In family therapy there is an emphasis on explaining families as behavioural and communication systems. An individual is not understood in his or her own terms. An individual is considered as part of a functioning whole and cannot be explained without reference to that whole. Throughout the research interviews, the feeling expressed was that, in therapy, individual members did not feel understood as either mothers or fathers, sons or daughters. The atmosphere, though intellectually correct, was emotionally arid. Behaviours were explained in the therapists' terms. They defined the situation. However, the feeling of individual members was that 'whereas I can be explained in your terms, I can only be *understood* in mine'. The therapeutic techniques were clinically sound but, as we heard in Chapter 4, they were felt to lack warmth and friendliness. Many of the families wanted a trusting relationship with the therapists before they were prepared or able to 'open up'. But they said that the method itself was a barrier. In short, most families felt explained but not understood. Indeed, no amount of explaining can ever produce an understanding of the subjective other. In some cases there was a longing to be understood but in the time-limited, task-orientated, cybernetically inspired workings of systemic family therapy such personal understanding, at least as most families experienced it, was not to be.

Again, we might recognize a two-way split: there were families who felt that they were understood by the therapists and there were families who felt that they were not understood by the therapists. However, the division is severely imbalanced with only a couple of families feeling that, in some way, the meaning of their personal experience was understood by the practitioners. The majority of families felt that they were not understood at this experiential level and, in a number of cases, this was perceived as a fundamental failure on the part of the therapists.

'We were understood'
For these families, explanation and understanding ran close companions. They said that the therapists had a good, accurate and useful understanding of their situation – 'they were on the right lines' – and this gave the families confidence. Mrs Roe said, 'It was nice to have someone who understood your troubles because it helped you feel that it just weren't you going crazy and that someone understood your point of view.' Mr Vassal reflected in similar vein:

> I felt that they got down to the nitty-gritty of what was wrong. They knew, like, what was going on so that . . . er . . . the way they put it, you knew you were coming across to them and they, like, in their way was coming across to us.

'We were not understood'
Most of the families who attended therapy felt that, at heart, they were not understood. At best, the technique gave the therapists a superficial picture and, at worst, it failed to sense the deep, personal distress experienced by individual family members. The method imposed a shallow template on their experience which confined their feelings and was unable to fathom the confusion, hurt and despair that swelled beneath some sessions, occasionally erupting in frustration and anger. In the eyes of the families, the technique seemed to overtake and interfere with the worker's ability to respond to personal feelings. Time and again, family members observed that the therapists did not appear to *listen* to them. They were too intent on 'firing questions', and they seemed to fail to listen to the answers. The focus of therapeutic interest kept changing and the personal experiences of individual family members was quickly lost in a blur of treatment interventions.

During the research interview, Mrs Ruff, in one of her quieter, more contemplative moments, said:

> 'I get very, very lonely on my own. I don't think anybody has ever

really understood my point of view, you know, how I feel and what it's
like for me. You see, I want a man; for him to be part of my family,
someone for me, for what I want but no one ever seem to understand
how it is.

Mrs Downs was the step-mother of Dean. He was not only getting
into trouble outside the home, he was very ambivalent about his
father's second wife. It was Mrs Downs who was 'having problems
with Dean. I try so hard with him but all I do is seem to get it all
wrong and make it worse.' Very close to tears, she continued to
explain how she felt:

> It had nearly come to blows between Dean and me. For me it was
> getting to be, you know, a really big problem. I couldn't stop thinking
> about it and it was really getting me all wound up. That's when I got
> in touch with the social services. I was so distressed. But that family
> therapy never really got on to how I felt, what I was really feeling, that
> I just couldn't handle it no more. More than anything I just wanted to
> sit down and talk with someone 'cos that would have helped, you know,
> but it wasn't like that. You had to . . . er . . . like, listen to them. They
> never listened to you as such. I just felt lost; upset, you know. It was
> hopeless really.

There was a long history of difficulties with the children in the
Pound family. Mrs Pound had four teenage children by her earlier
marriage and a baby daughter by her current relationship. Three
of the older children were in trouble of one kind or another, but
their mother's greatest worry was over Andrew, aged twelve. The
therapists were aware of the complexities and long-standing nature
of the problems that saturated the history of this disturbed family.
It appeared to Mrs Pound that most of their efforts, including those
of the child psychiatrist involved, went on trying to *explain* the
behaviour of the family and its members without anyone seeming
to be 'sympathetic' or 'helpful'.

It appeared to the therapists that the boundaries within the
Pound family were confused. The eldest child, aged sixteen, was
doing some of the work of a parent ('a parental child'). The initial
hypothesis was that 'Mum is victim and as such there is nothing
that she thinks she can do about taking charge of the children, and
in a way encourages them to be out of hand, because she feels
"boys should be boys". Her attempted solution is to bring in the
experts when what the boys really want is for her to take effective
control.' The aim, therefore, was 'to get Mum in control'. Along
with her boyfriend, various efforts were made to help Mrs Pound
feel less inadequate, more relaxed and confident in controlling her
children.

The fourth session revealed her considerable worries about

Andrew. Earlier in the year, Andrew had been indecently assaulted by a middle-aged man. His mother said:

> He took it very inwardly, and it must be disturbing him. I wanted him to see a psychiatrist. All the kids were taunting him at school and at home. I was hoping, in my way, they could probably put him out under hypnosis and get to the root of what was disturbing him because he couldn't talk about it. I think that he thought that there was something wrong with him. I was frightened that if things weren't brought out something would develop.

In the week prior to this fourth session, Mrs Pound caught Andrew exposing himself to his baby sister. She was worried that Andrew might have interfered with the baby at some time, but she was not sure. It emerged that, from being a young boy,

> Andrew always wanted nighties and petticoats and frilly knickers, handbags and dolls and things. He weren't a boy at all. He was very, very feminine. He giggle like a girl for everlasting in tears [sic]. He cried once when he told me that he was frightened that he was bisexual or homosexual and that is what I'm worried about. If . . . well,I know that if it is his way, that will be, like, but I want Andrew to be sorted out in his own mind whichever way in life he's going. . . . And you see I told them this, how worried I was, how upset I was and that one night I just wanted to talk with someone but they wouldn't come. They just put it back to the family therapy which in my eyes weren't settling anything when what I wanted was someone to help me think about everything especially what was happening to Andrew.

The therapists did acknowledge Mrs Pound's fears and arranged an urgent appointment for Andrew to see the psychiatrist. His conclusion

> . . . was that he does not suffer any diagnosable psychiatric disorder but along with the other children in the family is very disturbed as a result of the difficulties that they have all experienced. . . . The parental system is very confused and Kenny, the boyfriend, has a considerable distant relationship with Mrs Pound. I did feel quite strongly the main aim should be to improve that relationship and so provide the children with some stability but there seemed reluctance in that regard . . .

At the diagnostic interview the psychiatrist told Mrs Pound and Kenny that he saw no value in seeing Andrew on an individual basis: if Andrew's behaviour is going to change, they were told, then a family approach was needed, although they were warned by the psychiatrist that 'the going would be tough'. 'You and I,' wrote the psychiatrist to the social workers, 'decided that it would be most appropriate to see them all as a family and they agreed to this, but having made the appointment they failed to attend . . . I am sure they are going to re-appear with further problems.'

Mrs Pound picks up events as seen from her point of view:

I thought I weren't getting anywhere with any of them so I stopped going. I was upset, you know, I was actually angry to think I did ask for help and got nothing that I did feel helped. I did feel that this meeting as a family and everything was an interest of theirs, you know, something they liked doing. I didn't feel they really took any notice of how I was feeling . . . I feel they blamed me all the time. I know I'm not perfect. *I* know that, but they never got down to how any of us was . . . I felt misunderstood. Even now I feel upset about everything . . . I'm sorry . . . [Mrs Pound cried, and then after a few moments she recovered and continued] . . . In the past, there was one helpful one. He did make me feel as if he understood. If you had a problem he would listen, you know, as if he was really interested, like he could follow exactly what it was you were thinking.

At the time of the research interview, pain and sadness were still very much in evidence in a number of families for whom therapy had not felt a success. Luke's mother concluded:

No one really understood what we lived through. They never did really understand the situation. How badly it was upsetting us all. It was all too simple for our case. Just lots of questions. You answered one and boom! on to the next one. They never got to the bottom of anything. There was so much I wanted to say but I could never say it their way.

Luke had now left home. His mother continued:

I feel pretty sad about the way it all worked out. I still worry about him. He's on my mind from the minute I wake up in the morning till the minute I go to bed at night. Nine times out of ten I dream about him. Still, that's life, I suppose.

For most families who felt that they were not understood, at worst 'not to be understood' was deemed unfortunate, insensitive and regrettable. However, in the case of the Dooleys, it was judged to be harmful. Kent, aged fifteen, was at the centre of a complex web of family relationships in which his parents had both remarried. His mother and stepfather (Mr and Mrs Acres) could not cope with him. At various stages, Kent's father and wife (Mr and Mrs Dooley), and his maternal and paternal grandparents were all asked to join the sessions, or at least requested to consider the boy's future. Mr and Mrs Dooley recalled: 'We got a letter out of the blue to go to one of these meetings. We'd no idea what it was about or what had been going on. Looking back I was appalled.' The meetings, according to Mrs Dooley, were heated and ill-tempered and served nobody's interests:

Mrs D: Kent was bewildered. There he was in the middle with us all arguing who would or, more to the point, who did not want him. He looked in a state of shock.

Mr D: It all felt like an ultimatum about who should have Kent. It was all very pressured.

Mrs D: It was totally unreasonable. Imagine how poor bloody Kent felt with us all haggling who should, well in fact as I said, who didn't want him.

Mr D: It was all handled very insensitively.

Mrs D: I mean, couldn't they [the therapists] imagine what it must have felt like for that boy.

Mr D: Very blunt. Tactless really.

Mrs D: I really was disgusted about the way everything was put. All Kent was hearing from them was 'Well, your Mum doesn't want you, your Dad doesn't want you, and maybe your Gran doesn't so you'll have to go into care!' Can you imagine!

Mr D: We were all made to feel guilty. But you see, coming out of thin air, as it did, we didn't have time to make a decision on the spot which is almost what they were asking.

Mrs D: The whole thing caused a great deal of upset between Martin and me. We're not over it yet, are we? It's made things very rocky between us. In fact we have thought about splitting up – all over this.

Mr D: What we needed was time to think through what they were asking, not given two days to make a major decision. We needed some kind of counselling but we were told it all had to take place in the meetings. In fact we now need some counselling because of the meetings and what they did!

Mrs D: Couldn't they [the therapists] just have stopped and thought what they were doing by throwing us all together like that. Feelings were running very high, you know. At one stage I thought I was heading for a nervous breakdown. I felt in an impossible position.

Accounts and understandings

Each occasion of family therapy was under the control of the therapists. It was they who determined the direction and set the tone, asked the questions and made the observations. What family members said and did was in response to the therapist. The situation was defined in terms prescribed by the therapeutic team. The character of replies and the behaviour of family members was built into the structure of the occasion. What was said and done could not be a totally free expression on the part of each individual. It was triggered and set within the framework of family therapy, and its meaning was couched in the idiom of systems theory. A family had no power to introduce an alternative definition. In other words, what took place in a session was not a free-floating event to which the therapist responded. What transpired had to occur within the conceptual and behavioural parameters laid down in the therapist's definition of what sort of things should happen on occasions of this kind. There was a 'construct' of family therapy into which responses were 'cued'.

There is no neutral description available of 'just what happened' in therapy. Rather, the therapist gives an 'account' of what happened which is perceived through the 'construct' of family therapy. Events are accommodated within the predetermined schemata which, in this case, is a systemic account of how families as a whole function and how internal parts relate and communicate. Such constructs do two things: (i) they constrain and direct what takes place; and (ii) having evoked responses according to the vocabulary of the construct, they are available for, and amenable to, being 'accounted'. The whole show, including the style and content, is under the therapist's direction. The therapist's explanation holds because the evidence that feeds into the explanation is already phrased in the language of that construct. If a family wishes to talk in a different language, it will be either ignored or forbidden, recast or simply not understood. The occasion is that of systematic family therapy and all exchanges and transactions take place in its currency.

Thus, the argument is that systemic family therapy is not a construct which is able to understand individual personal experience. A personal experience is foreign to the properties of that construct. If an individual wishes his personal experience to be understood, it will not be intelligible within the language of family therapy. Those who wish to speak outside the construct of systemic family therapy have to speak outside the context of family therapy. The method is locked into a different set of signals which are read for a different purpose. It does not hear the subjectivity of the other. This may be why many families failed to recognize their social worker when he or she turned therapist. And if we are to believe England and Williams, the inability to describe and experience not only frustrates being understood, it denies the individual the ability to make sense of what is happening to them and inhibits their attempt to organize an understanding of their world. Without a construct which allows the communication of personal experience, the personal reality of the individual is more difficult to maintain.

7 Verdicts

There is no one yardstick by which to measure a welfare service. The measures used depend on the assumptions made by practitioners and sponsors, recipients and researchers. These assumptions might be identified in the answers given to the following three areas of questioning. First, what is the purpose of the practice? What aims does it pursue? How should things look when the practice is complete? This is matter of ideology. Normative questions are raised. Second, how is the situation to be understood and explained? The answer to this question depends on the theoretical outlook of those involved and entails epistemological issues. Third, how do you find out what is happening and how do you do something about it? These are questions of methodology. Ideology, epistemology and methodology colour the assumptions of both the practitioner and the researcher and lead to knotty problems when the two meet. I need to reveal the sorts of measurements I have been taking before announcing the verdicts.

Built into the research style was a preference for appreciating the experiences of the consumer rather than taking measurements of the behaviour of the problem child. This preference is premissed on the belief that, in human affairs, the subjective experience and the personal outlook of the participants has to be understood if people and their behaviour are to make sense. Describing what people say and do in objective terms may form the basis of an explanation but it does not produce an understanding. The research focus and style employed in this study encourage verdicts to be announced in the words of family members as they reflect on their experience of family therapy. However, we can also introduce measures of a different kind. A few observations can be made on the behaviour of the problem child before and after family therapy. We can add, too, some broad economic judgements such as the cost of family therapy in terms of time, effort and money. I shall weave these behavioural and economic judgements into the experiential reports, although the part they play remains subdued and less strident, given the prevailing design of the research.

When discussing the value, usefulness and effectiveness of

therapy, families offered two kinds of judgement. The first was a verdict on whether or not family therapy has had any desirable effect on the problem that originally brought them to social services. The second was a comment on the method of treatment itself. We shall consider each of these in turn.

Impact on the behaviour of the 'problem' child

In most cases, a family came to therapy because a parent or the parents felt that they were having problems with the behaviour of one of their children. The general feeling was that the child was beyond their control and that family life was becoming thoroughly miserable. The behaviours most commonly exhibited by the difficult child included lying and rudeness, aggression and disobedience, theft and truancy. At interview, the majority of parents said that family therapy had been without beneficial effect, but there were a few exceptions and we shall consider their views first.

Three families felt that, on the whole, therapy had helped. Mr and Mrs Vassal, who completed treatment, were in no doubt: 'It did him [Peter, their son] a lot of good,' said Mr Vassal. 'He's grown up a bit more. He's taken up fishing which has taken the boredom out of him a bit,' added Mrs Vassal. Mr Vassal then reflected, 'Peter just improved out of the blue, sudden like. Whether they got through to him by him having to keep going down there when he couldn't be bothered, I don't know, but it did the trick.' Peter was still behaving himself a year later.

The Clarks also completed the full course of treatment. They felt that things were better. Karen, who had been staying out late, mixing with a 'rough crowd' and drinking, had curbed her excesses.

> *Mr C:* One of the reasons we went there was that she wasn't taking any notice of us, shouting and swearing at us and so on and things got very turbulent on both sides. No one was listening to me. Mother and daughter weren't able to communicate. I think as a result of going to them things are better. Are they? [to Karen] Only you can tell us.
>
> *Mrs C:* See-saws a bit but things are a bit better.
>
> *Karen:* I think it's better than before we went. We don't have so many rows. We can talk a lot better. Before the meetings I felt it was them, always getting at me. But I can see it's me as well.

Unfortunately, a few months later Karen, approaching her seventeenth birthday, committed several offences including theft and criminal damage for which she was charged.

A couple of families did say that matters had improved, but

insisted that this was due to their own efforts and not the result of treatment. 'Everything's fine at home now,' said Mrs Kegg. 'But what we did at home ourselves was ten times more use than what they did.' However, within the year, their daughter Emma, now almost seventeen, had left home to live with her boyfriend and together they had committed a number of offences, including theft.

For the majority of families, matters had not improved. At the time of the research interview they were still reporting difficulties with their 'problem' child as well as upsets elsewhere in family life. However, one mother despite her daughter's continued awkward behaviour, did feel that she coped better as a result of family therapy: 'I mean with Louise, things aren't any better. She's not changed, but I try to approach it from a different angle, to stand back a bit. . . . They highlighted . . . I mean, I'd already figured out the right form of action but they helped me see that I was on the right lines, if you see what I mean.'

The overwhelming verdict was captured in a phrase that cropped up in almost every interview with those families who felt dissatisfied: 'it was a waste of time.' At best, the problem behaviours were no better and, at worst, they had deteriorated. Sixteen year-old Luke continued shoplifting and left home before the end of treatment. In his mother's words:

> After that we didn't see the point in any more family therapy. Looking back I now believe it couldn't have really worked – although I wouldn't have said this at one time – but I think that whatever is in them genetically, you know, because Luke's adopted and his father was a bad lot, whatever is in them will come out. He is the way he is and he can't help that and I don't blame him for it. It's just very sad.

Also 'looking back', Mrs Pound said 'I felt completely disappointed. It just seemed a complete waste of time. Things are no better; in fact they're worse.' Mrs Pound, who was already anticipating the court appearance of two of her boys, later learned that Andrew, aged twelve, had been caught by the police for theft and then again, a few weeks later, he was found handling stolen goods.

Two mothers decided to force the hand of the social services department. They felt that their children were beyond their control and they wanted them received into care. This is how Mrs Needham tells her story:

> We'd had a few of these family sessions but then Tracey got worse. She got into more trouble with the boys, spending nights out and all sorts and so I called them again and they said try some more of this

therapy thing and I said 'It didn't work the first time so it won't work now.' 'Oh,' they said 'it did work the first time because she's been good' which was nothing to do with them because she has her ups and downs. Anyway, we did go back because we had no choice but Tracey got worse. Well one afternoon I was completely desperate. I took her down to the office and left her there! I said, 'Now you look after her.' I said 'when I wanted help you wouldn't give it me and now she's on drugs, sniffing things'. . . . Well they took her to her nanny's which was stupid because she pinched all her jewellery and flogged it in the city. . . . Anyway she ended up in a children's home. The therapy did not achieve anything. To be honest, now that Tracey's in care, life is much better for all of us.

Mrs Ruff, in somewhat more colourful language, told a similar tale. Wayne's behaviour was beyond her control and comprehension. She wanted him removed and treated and did not feel that family therapy was the way to achieve these ends:

They kept wanting Wayne's brother there and we weren't getting anywhere. I felt really angry so I says 'I've had a fucking 'nough of this'. I said 'if you're not bloody well going to help him then I'm wasting my fucking time here, ain't I' and he said 'Well, to be honest, yes'. 'Well,' I said, 'Thank you for fucking nothing,' and I said 'When I get home I'm going to kill that little bastard Wayne.' Well, of course [she smiles], they thought I meant it. Well when I got home here, there was a social worker already been round taking a Place of Safety Order, a twenty-eight day thing it was, because they said the little bugger was in danger! I had to laugh! He's now on a Care Order.

Mrs Ruff said that 'Wayne loves it in care'. She described the home as 'a beautiful place. Too good for him!' Yet, despite her assessment, she added 'But now he's done a runner. He got in with a bad crowd and they stole a car. You see there's not enough punishment where he is. They're too soft.' Indeed, Wayne's tumble down the slippery slope continued unabated. After a series of offences including robbery and theft he was placed on a two-year supervision order which included 120 hours community work and six 'weekend' sentences under the supervision and direction of social workers specializing in work with adolescents. Three months later, while home on trial, Wayne stole a car, broke bail and went to a prison remand centre before finally receiving 28 weeks of youth custody.

It is difficult to give an exact 'behavioural' picture of what happened to parents and their children during the twelve months after therapy. Many of the young people had reached ages of sixteen and seventeen years and would not necessarily have come to the attentions of social services and their files even if they had continued to misbehave. A few families vowed never to return to the 'welfare'. However, at least as far as the department's records were concerned, out of the eleven original 'non-takers', four had received visits from social workers in connection with offences committed by their children, with one child eventually committed to local authority care. Of the twenty-three families who had experienced therapy, four of the 'problem' children had left home. Two were committed to local authority care, although, as we have heard, Wayne Ruff was actually in youth custody. A third child was technically in care, but he was being fostered by his grandparents. Three sets of 'parents' were known to have split up, with one couple already in the throes of divorce proceedings. Including those who had left home or who were in care, during the twelve months since the last session of family therapy, fourteen of the originally identified 'problem' children had committed offences which had brought them to the notice of the police.

The experience of family therapy

Irrespective of family therapy's impact on the problem behaviour, six families felt, in the words of one mother, that the idea of 'sitting down and talking like that was good'. She continued: 'Like, sometimes people don't admit things to each other and they help you get it out in the open.' Mr Vassal said, 'The way they put it over to you, it sunk in. I'd return there if things got bad, certainly, yes, it was very useful.' Mrs Downs believed that 'Through talking we all realized it all came through me and my boyfriend, so in a way it was a good thing. The talk did more good than anything. . . . I would go back I suppose if things ever got bad again.'

The remaining families did not value their experience of family therapy and would not return. For some, it did not match their expectations: 'I was expecting someone to come round straight away 'cos I desperately needed to see someone.' For others, family therapy was either not as good as other kinds of help which had been received in the past – 'Now that young policeman was good. He spent ages listening to us and calming us down' – or it was as bad as previous experiences of being helped – 'It was as bad as that psychiatrist at child guidance. We got nowhere with him either.'

Mr and Mrs Spree, like a number of parents, wanted someone to talk to their daughter and deliver some kind of check and official admonishment to their difficult offspring:

> Mrs S: We wanted them to say to her 'Look, it's not on to speak like that, so rude and awkward to everyone. It's unreasonable and upsets everyone.' We wanted someone like a family doctor that knew us and that we could get in touch with easily and chat with if we needed them.
>
> Mr S: We wanted her to know that she is worth something and we do care about her. Their way, the way they did it was too remote. It felt like a mountain out of a molehill situation. Sledgehammer for nuts, sort of thing.
>
> Mrs S: It was far too intense.
>
> Mr S: They made it a major event which made it worse.
>
> Mrs S: In fact it was the health visitor, the one I phoned first of all when I was so desperate, it was her who was good. She was wonderful. She was really, really nice. So understanding. Really reassuring. She came over straight away. We had a cup of tea and that was really nice and she listened and I felt better and I suppose I was expecting them to be a bit like that.

In the main, families held two kinds of expectation. One was that some practical or verbal advice would be offered. This might include offering a temporary break from the child or, in the less desperate cases, giving a few instructions about how to handle an obstreperous teenager. The other hope was that someone would listen and that they would understand what was happening. This was usually expressed in variations of the phrase 'I wanted them to come round, sit down, have a nice cup of tea and a chat' which was heard again and again during the course of the study. Mrs Ruff compared the family therapist with Simon, 'an ordinary social worker', who visited her.

> Now he showed care for people, he did, and they [the family therapists] don't want to know that. They've got to keep distant. I can't confide in them like I could with Simon. He'd sit down, have a natter and help you. . . . They're a load of crap. A bunch of wankers is what Wayne called them, didn't you?

Although the children themselves tended not to be as expansive in their comments as their parents, nevertheless their judgements were less varied and generally quite unambiguous. 'Boring', 'stupid' and, again, 'a waste of time' were typical verdicts. But, of anyone, it was the men – as husbands, fathers and stepparents – who were slightly more likely to give the technique of family therapy the benefit of any doubts that they might have. We have already encountered this in the case of Mr Kegg and Mr Clark who, compared to their wives, were not so hostile to the experience. The systematic way in which the therapists went about their work seemed to appeal: 'They got everyone to state their point of view. They set out things fairly, you know, building up a picture of how we were. I thought that was useful.' These comments echo the findings of Zuk (1978) who noted that, whereas women and children emphasized whole emotional experiences when trying to understand their situation, men tended to stress the need for rationality and efficiency, orderliness and the adherence to rules when analysing their situation. For three fathers, the shift of attention away from them as individuals on to the whole family was a welcome change in focus. 'Whereas before', felt Mr Bond, 'I seemed to get the blame for everything which really wasn't accurate, they obviously saw it as something that all of us were involved in and it was not productive to keep loading the blame on to one person. It avoided the real issue.'

Nevertheless, in spite of these mellower judgements, most families did not like family therapy as a method of help. They voted with their feet and did not return. Of those who started therapy, 71 per cent failed to complete the prescribed course of treatment. The effect of people not keeping appointments had serious consequences for how efficiently the therapists were able to use their time. Over a seventeen-month period beginning in April 1985 and excluding the team's 'study and theory' days, the therapists had a total of 236 individual sessions available to see families: 139 (59 per cent) of these were 'booked' for particular families; of these 139 appointments, 85 (61 per cent) were kept by the families. Or looked at another way, out of the 236 theoretically available sessions, 85 (36 per cent) were actually used. This explained why there were more than the customary one or two observers for each family seen. It also went some way to explain why families were wont to describe the observers as 'the committee' or 'the panel'. In the language of systems theory, something of a positive feedback loop set in: families felt uncomfortable being observed by a large number of anonymous therapists and so they failed to keep their next appointment. This released the therapists to join their colleagues and thus they were able to observe another family.

Operating at maximum efficiency, a family would normally be treated by one therapist, a superviser and an observer. Including preparation and debriefing time, one family session might consume 2 hours. At 1986 prices for a level 3 social worker, the cost of this one session works out at approximately £45.40. This figure excludes the slightly higher cost of the team leader and administrative expenses such as the typing of letters and records, filing, and the workers' travel costs. It also excludes the time given by the consultant psychiatrist which, as far as the researcher was aware, came free to social services. However, if we cost the price of all the weekly afternoon sessions, whether or not families appeared, the cost of one session for a family *actually* seen rises to £147.50.

Conclusion

On the whole, these are harsh verdicts, whether judged on experiential, behavioural or economic grounds. However, the judgements bear further examination, particularly at the ideological and theoretical level, less to soften the blow but more to understand the difficult position in which social workers find themselves. The families with which the therapists worked were often highly disturbed, torn and unhappy. By most standards, many were 'heavy-end' cases, several of which had also 'failed' at the hands of psychiatrists and clinical psychologists from the local child guidance clinic. What, then, are the implications of this enquiry? And second, in the light of the understandings reached, what lessons emerge for social workers wishing to work with families in a local authority setting? Clearly the answers to the second question depend on how we respond to the first. In Part III we tackle such questions and explore the nature of the answers.

PART III

POWER AND SUBJECTIVITY IN FAMILY THERAPY

8 The power of the therapist

The task of this chapter is to discover what therapists hear when they listen to families reflecting on their experiences of systemic based therapy. We must recognize that the client's word is not taken at face value by all those who are asked to pay heed. First, I shall mount a modest defence on behalf of the therapists before slipping over to the other side and throwing in my lot with those who gain inspiration from practices based on humanist principles. Such apparent treachery does not result from some sentimental attachment to the underdog but arises from certain theoretical views held about the nature of social reality and those who are set to experience it.

In my enquiries so far, two worlds have been brought face-to-face. One is that of the systemic family therapist who explains the family in terms of a set of relationships and communication exchanges. The other is that of the family and its members who personally experience the efforts of the therapist and harbour subjective views of that experience. It is by no means a straightforward matter to give either one of these worlds primacy over the other, at least in epistemological terms. Politically, of course, it is a different matter. In the therapeutic encounter, most of the power appears to lie with the therapist. This is why those who discover the views of the consumer find themselves arguing for client 'empowerment' in an attempt to redress the balance. But this is to anticipate a later line of thought. At this stage we need to consider how the objective world of the therapist and the subjective world of the consumer (as revealed by the researcher) account for each other's character and performance. In particular, I shall describe the various reactions available to the systemic family therapist in which she 'explains' the reasons for families saying what they say and doing what they do. Depending on your point of view, such accounts may be read as either explanations or rationalizations. Along this route we shall describe three defensive positions. The first sees the family as a group capable of stout behavioural resistance. The second blames the therapeutic strategy but not the underlying principles. The third, and ultimately the most robust, denies the validity of the evidence called to challenge the case for family therapy.

Families who resist

The behaviour of families who break appointments or leave therapy or fail to carry out the instructions of the therapist may be seen as further evidence of their pathological condition. In other words, the criticisms which families make of therapy simply indicate a failure on their part to change established habits of relating. Change can be painful. Indeed, the greater the change needed, the greater will be the effort required. On the whole, pain and effort are to be avoided, unless individuals see benefits on the horizon. Resistance, according to the therapist, is simply an unwillingness to change. It means that the therapist is getting close to important but painful areas. Flight from the cause of such threatened pain is the instinctive course of action. It is not surprising that some families leave therapy. The therapist may observe that 'The family was not ready to change' or 'The family did not wish to be helped' or 'Clearly, the family is denying the problem'.

In systemic terms, the concept of homeostasis offers a straightforward explanation of resistance. Systems seek to maintain themselves in a state of equilibrium. Change, embodied in the activities of the therapist, threatens to disturb this equilibrium. Thus, there is an inbuilt resistance to change. So, of course, families who fail to take advantage of therapy are bound to say the things they say. It is not an indictment of therapy. It is further confirmation of the family's pathological mode of functioning.

Owning the failure

However, the family therapist who embraces a systems approach to the full is made of stronger stuff. Undaunted, her systemic analysis must conclude that families who leave therapy or fail to change are merely giving a further demonstration of their system's characteristic properties. The failure to find an effective way into this system and change its pattern lies entirely with the therapist. The family cannot be blamed. The therapist needs to consider what it is that the family is resisting. What changes are they keeping at bay? The resisting itself can indicate the mechanisms which the family system uses to maintain its present pattern of functioning. The task of the therapist is to refine her analysis and look for better and more imaginative routes into the apparent impasse. The joint system of family *and* therapist has to be 'reframed' in order that the pattern of relationships makes better sense.

A favourite ploy used by the therapist at this stage is to employ a paradox. This is how Minuchin and Fishman (1981, p. 244–5) lead up to the technique:

Our use of paradox is based on an understanding of three concepts: the concept of the family as a self-regulatory system, the concept of the system as a mechanism for self regulation, and the concept of systemic resistance to change, resulting from the preceding two. Because the symptom is used to regulate a dysfunctional part of the system, if the symptom is eliminated, that part of the system will be left unregulated. The most common example of this is parents who divert their conflict through a child's activating a symptom. In alleviating the symptom in the child, the therapist allows the unresolved issues between the parents to become exposed, creating a great deal of anxiety and a strong resistance to change. We use paradox primarily as a clinical tool for dealing with this resistance and circumventing a power struggle between the family and therapist. Families with symptomatic children usually present the therapist with a contradictory request, asking that the symptom be changed without changing their system. The therapist deals with this contradiction through a series a drastic redefinitions that connect the sympton with the system in such a way that one cannot be changed without changing the other.

By owning the failure when a family leaves therapy, the worker can explain the resistance, think of better ways of working in the future and preserve the explanatory power of a systems approach. The theory is not at fault. Failures are simply a measure of the worker's limitations in understanding and applying her techniques.

A clash in epistemology and methodology
So far, the systemic family therapist has listened to what families have had to say on the assumption that both the family and the therapist occupy the same universe of meaning. As far as the therapist is concerned, the client's utterances are understood in the language of systems theory. As we have heard, some therapists explain criticism in terms of simple resistance. More reflective therapists recognize the powerful inertia built into all homeostatic mechanisms. They blame themselves for failing to realign relationships. So, although hearing what families have to say about therapy is a sobering experience, it reminds therapists how much further they have to go in refining and honing their techniques and practices. At no time does the therapist step outside the systems frame of reference.

However, it is possible to adopt an altogether more truculent posture. Rather than be reasonable and allow the client to speak in this way, the systemic family therapist could argue that the kind of information identified as forming the consumer's view has nothing worthwhile to say to the applied behavioural scientist. The character of the data is not acceptable. The position adopted is similar to that of the experimental psychologist confronted with the findings of an astrologer. The psychologist would not be worried unduly by the charge of wilfully ignoring the patterns made by the stars, the conjunction of planets and the part played by birth signs when assessing personality types. Similarly, those who seek the views and experiences of families who have undergone therapy could be said to misunderstand fundamentally the way in which systems theory explains and tackles family behaviour. The data that should be collected concern the observed patterns of behaviour and communication that families use to relate within their social system. Such methods of data collection look to the natural sciences for their inspiration. People and their situations are seen as objects possessing certain characteristics which can be observed, described and quantified. The social world, like the physical, has an external existence which is objectively available for those who wish to examine it. In this objective sense there is a search for order, regularity and causal links between phenomena. At this stage, we can profitably remind ourselves that the systemic family therapist prefers to argue that behaviour produces experience and not the other way round. Therefore a catalogue of unhappy therapeutic experiences merely confirms that such families are still urgently needing to change the behavioural characteristics of their family system. In this tougher mood, the family therapist places no intrinsic value on the client's point of view. It is merely a product of the family system and its current mode of functioning.

Of course, there is a similar presumption on the part of the researcher who collects such viewpoints and experiences, although here matters are reversed. The qualitative researcher approaches social reality assuming that the way to understand people is to look at the world from their point of view. There is no level of meaning beyond and above the individual's subjective consciousness. The systemic family therapist reifies the family and gives it physical properties that appear to transcend individual members. Subjectivists reject this stance. They believe that the job of those who wish to make sense of people is to understand their subjective experience. The task is to discover what situations *mean* to those who participate. Those who remain on the outside of personal experience see only objects behaving or systems functioning which may be fine for explaining bricks falling or machines working, but it is no way to understand human beings.

However, there is a conceptual snag in all of this. It involves a curious, yet challenging, methodological oddity. Introduced in the form of a question, we might ask 'What are the nature, status and relationship between data obtained from a qualitative and experientially based enquiry and a scientifically styled therapeutic technique?' Can a subjective methodology be used to evaluate an objective epistemology? Is the consumer in a position to comment sensibly and appropriately on the expertise of the producer? The assumptions about the nature of human beings and their behaviour differ fundamentally between the research strategy and the treatment method. What, if anything, can the findings of an interpretivist enquiry say to those who practise behavioural programmes of treatment? The unabashed answer from the unrepentant systemic family therapist is that the experiences of the consumer, though anecdotally amusing, say little of scientific value. Seeking the views of the subject and changing practice in the light of those views produce a person-centred family therapy. But can such a thing exist?

Systemic family therapy does not conceive of the family as a group of individuals with independent and discrete personal characteristics. The level of explanation is the family system and its overall pattern of relating. It begins to sound as if a humanistic, person-centred systemic family therapy is a hybrid destined to be stillborn – the unlikely product of an impossible union between wilfully independent performers on the stage of human affairs. Systemic family therapists may make certain concessions towards the concept of subjectivity, but if they travel but a short way down this road they cease to be that which they profess.

There can be no real communication between these two camps. The assumptions built into their respective positions differ fundamentally. Rojek (1986) has a stirring image in which theoreticians of the objective and subjective persuasion behave like gladiators, battling unto death to see whose epistemology is the stronger. In this war of words the protagonists believe that a winner will emerge. But there will be no winner. Barbs are aimed at targets whose existence is denied by the intended victim. The weapons of each side are judged impotent by the other. They make no sense once outside their own frame of reference. In effect, the qualitative researcher cannot be understood by the behavioural practitioner while, conversely, the behavioural practitioner can make no sense of the interpretivist who looks to the world of personal meaning for his or her understanding of people and their situations.

The place of the consumer study in the evaluation of systemic family therapy therefore raises interesting questions. We need to clear a path through some of this tangle in order to reach less cluttered ground. One way of proceeding is to recognize that the various parties involved sponsor views that reflect, indeed support, their particular interests (for a fuller version of this idea see Howe, 1987). Each interest implies a definition of welfare work with families which entails a basic purpose. The success of family work is measured in terms of whether or not the favoured purpose is achieved. This is reasonably straightforward in the case of the practitioner and the consumer. When we define the practitioner as someone who uses certain techniques to bring about objective behavioural changes in an identified client system, practice is evaluated in terms of whether the specified behaviours did or did not change in the manner predicted. The encounter is between the practitioner and the client, with the practitioner controlling the content and direction of practice.

On the other hand, we have also recognized that there are those who think that the views and experiences of clients are the measure by which social work efforts have to be judged. It is the quality of the encounter between worker and client that is valued and not any crude behavioural outcome determined by the worker. There is a shift from measuring the 'problem behaviour' to understanding the 'person in trouble'.

However, it is also possible to evaluate matters qualitatively by seeking the views and experiences of those who *produce* welfare and therapy. How do they, as practitioners, feel about family therapy? Do they enjoy it? Do they think that it is worthwhile? Rather than assess consumer satisfaction, it is possible to judge a service by the commitment and enthusiasm it engenders in those who provide it. Happy workers are good workers, and it may well be that a good worker is an effective worker. Family therapy scores high marks in its ability to produce worker interest, commitment and satisfaction. Social workers who practise family therapy do unusual things like read professionally relevant books, attend conferences and workshops and develop support groups. Family therapy appears to offer social workers a clear, coherent theoretical package with useful prescriptions for practice. Fellow travellers include psychiatrists and psychologists and they are good company to keep for those concerned about their professional image. The morale of family therapists is relatively high and so managers are likely to be in favour of a technique that produces a hardworking, enthusiastic and contented workforce. In fact, family therapy is a good antidote to the fashionable malady, burn-out, which is generally regarded as a reaction to stress in the work environment. 'Agencies and clients,' writes Zastrow (1984, p. 154), 'are shortchanged by professionals who have burned out.' Any practice that revives the worker's energies must attract the interest and support of any manager who is alert to the emotional condition of his or her workforce.

It is along this line of thought that we meet those who believe that much welfare work is essentially designed to promote the interests and meet the needs of professional workers. Social workers are part of what Renner (1953) has called the 'services classes' and Gould (1980) has dubbed the 'salaried middle classes' (SMC). Gould, amongst others, has suggested that the SMC are the prime beneficiaries of increased social provision and state activity. In this analysis, not only are welfare bureaucracies run *by* the SMC but it is run *for* them too. The SMC have 'the ability to act in their own interests' (Gould, 1980, p. 410). Thus, family therapists, at least in this context, are a group who amply demonstrate the ability of the SMC to define needs and how they are to be met in such a way as to suit their own occupational skills and professional interests. Family therapy is an example of a strategy and technique that reflects the self-interested nature of a particular service class. The environment which the family therapists address is perceived and defined in the light of professional interests. The family therapist does not respond to the personally experienced condition of the family itself, but rather to the family as defined by the concepts and technology of systems theory. The professional imposes her meaning on the family and its behaviour. She has the power to control both what the problem situation means and how it shall be tackled.

Thus, there is no necessary overlap in the hopes and purposes of those who seek help, those who offer expert practices and those who manage social statutes and policies. Families may want a personal service, therapists may attempt to change behaviours by changing families, while managers aim to keep children out of expensive care provision and welcome any technique that holds out the possibility of allowing children to remain with their parents. It is therefore possible to succeed by one measure yet fail by another. And just to add one more twist in this complicated affair, each purpose and its supporting rationale lends itself to a particular method of evaluation. Each purpose and its associated method of evaluation reflects the outlook and interests, beliefs and values of those whose sponsor a particular version of welfare work.

The position adopted in the present research enquiry was to try to understand how things looked from the family's point of view. I now return to this position although, in the light of the current discussion, it can be seen that this is one amongst several possible standpoints. However, it is strong ground to occupy and it can be bolstered further by appealing to arguments which assert that any personal social service must personally satisfy those who seek that service. But, in adopting this position, I realize fully that there may be no common ground between the researcher who values personal experiences and the practitioner who seeks behavioural changes. In effect, if the subjectivist and the objectivist remain unmoved, the business of one has no relevance to the concerns of the other. There are those who attempt to discover 'meta-positions' which transcend these factional squabbles but, though very attractive, they involve advanced theorizing which would take us beyond the brief of this book. Choosing to go the way of the interpretivist implies a critique of systemic family therapy. So, although the following arguments hold that the experiences of clients merit serious consideration and are therefore highly partisan, nevertheless they do allow me to promote a form of practice which has definite and sharp outlines. In order to reach this version of family social work we need first to make two observations. One notes the power of the therapist to render the family as an entity amenable to treatment. The second recognizes that, in the face of such professional power, pockets of resistance emerge; families fight those who attempt to impose an alien reality on their way of seeing things. They may not always be successful but they point the way to an alternative form of family practice which takes into account the family's version of events and their need to have some control over the content and direction of help.

The knowledge and power of the family therapist
At this stage we return to themes first introduced in Chapter 1: the formation of the family as both an object of social policy and a vehicle for socialization and treatment. Family therapists arise as part of this 'formation'. They perpetuate and develop the field of the 'family' in a way which confirms their particular perspective. The family takes on its form in the domain of what Donzelot (1979) calls the 'social'. The social emerges between the private and the public and covers that area of behaviour which causes public concern and yet has its roots in personal relations. It allows the state to penetrate the world of private relations insofar as they bear on public conduct, and in turn, personal behaviour develops in ways which take into account social expectations of how an individual should act. In this way, the state has taken an interest in many aspects of family life, including the quality of child-rearing and child behaviour. Thus, in the same social act, the state, or at least those employed to foster its concerns, both identifies a behaviour as unacceptable and proffers a course of action (treatment and education) to remedy the condition. Harris and Webb (1987)

repeatedly and deliberately explore this dual force, particularly as it relates to the 'socialisation of the deviant young'. In their exposition these authors track how delinquency becomes a subject of welfare concern and how welfare needs become the object of judicial appraisal:

> The discipline of the social . . . represents in one sense an extension of the function of classical law from proscription to prescription. The law prohibits certain kinds of child abuse and neglect, but the social professionals teach positive child-rearing . . . (p. 69)

> In the personal social services, consumers may be either beneficiaries of a service or its targets; more frequently they are both simultaneously. (p. 47)

The social is territory patrolled by those who hold both perspectives in view – those of welfare and legal judgement. In this very broad sense, they are 'social' workers. Family therapists are a particular breed of social worker and, as their name suggests, the family earns their special attention as a place where behaviour emerges and where it can be treated. Surveillance and regulation, diagnosis and treatment, proscription and prescription form the subtle, chimerical world of the social worker. The favourite metaphors of those who write about the family as it exists in the domain of the social is to see it as under a form of clinical and judicial attack. Donzelot sees the family as 'encircled', 'invaded' and 'colonised'. Lasch (1977) describes it as 'beseiged'. Cohen talks of the family group being 'penetrated' and 'occupied' by a series of experts in human relations. No longer is it the case that the aberrant individual is absorbed by the institutions of society, but rather the community institutions of medicine and psychiatry, law and punishment have been absorbed by the systems of formal control (Cohen, 1985, p. 78)

Over the centuries we have seen the object of punitive and remedial attention shift away from the body to the mind. From inflicting pain on the flesh there has been a move towards treating the psyche. In his discussion of Foucault, Cohen describes how

> The new power was not to punish less but to punish better, to punish more deeply into the social body. A new army of technicians (wardens, doctors, chaplains, psychiatrists, educators, social workers, criminologists, penologists) took over from the executioner (the 'immediate anatomist of pain') and proceeded to provide theories which would justify punishment as an exercise in changing the mind . . . the subject was to be observed, retrained and rendered obedient, not just punished along some abstract scale of justice. (1985, pp. 25–6)

However, changing people and their psychologies proved to be peculiarly difficult, and attention was directed towards taking one further step. Modern 'social control talk' marks a reaction against treating the mind to changing the 'act'. In this approach, behaviours and patterns of interaction (and *not* the intentions that lay behind them) are altered and realigned in order to produce conformity. It is not the intention to bring light, reason and insight into the minds of wrongdoers, rather it is a demand that they change their *behaviour* in ways decreed by those who intervene. 'External compliance' and not 'internal insight' have become the new aims. 'The offender is not asked to change, but to show an ability to maintain the overt demands of a conforming life. The stress is on retraining and providing skills; the delinquent is someone who has not learnt the rules of the social game' (Cohen, 1985, p. 145). It is no coincidence that much of this sounds like systemic family therapy. Both have strong behavioural roots. The therapist is someone who asserts that she possesses knowledge about the way families work – whether for the social good or the public ill. And if we add to this the aphorism that 'knowledge is power', we begin to recognize the therapist as someone whose particular type of knowledge brings her a special type of power in family affairs. But, as Foucault reminds us, it is misleading to see power as an oppressive, limiting thing:

> We must cease once and for all to describe the effects of power in negative terms: it 'excludes', it 'represses', it 'censors', it 'abstracts', it 'masks', it 'conceals'. In fact, power produces; it produces reality; it produces domains of objects and rituals of truth. (quoted in Cohen, 1985, p. vi)

Those who hold power have the ability to define situations, shape experiences and design futures. For example, Davis (1986) demonstrates how a client's initial version of her 'troubles' is transformed within the course of a 45-minute therapy session into a problem suitable for psychotherapeutic work. 'The problem,' she concludes, 'becomes viewable as a construction, requiring considerable work on the part of the therapist. His main activity, in fact, resides in persuading the client to accept the problem, as defined by him' (ibid., p. 70). Knowledge of the social and what constitutes its fluid, Janus-like properties gives the social worker a distinct advantage over others who find themselves exhibiting their private world in the domain of the public. Social workers and therapists can anchor their thoughts where others drift in confusion and uncertainty. Such rocks of conceptual solidity attract all those seeking a grip on events. The family therapist can explain what is happening and she can say what is to be done. She can 'make sense' where others find only no sense. Harris and Webb give us a good flavour of this in their discussion of juvenile delinquency:

The offender may indulge in sexual misdemeanour or torture animals, be too fond of fires or have a predilection for placing boulders on railway lines. Such behaviour is literally senseless to the magistrate whose explanatory framework allows principally for motivation-instigated criminality; nor is it quite satisfactory to consider it one of the acceptable mysteries of growing up. Again the experts translate such *bizarrerie* into a language which, if not fully comprehensible to the layman, at least gives an indication that somebody understands what is going on ... Indeed so neatly can an expert's report launder a complex and messy reality that it can make the precise details of the youngster's offence seem almost to have been predestined from the day of conception. (1987, pp. 84–5).

But there is another point of profound importance which must be added. It has to be remembered that professionals are not people who simply discover that they have knowledge over certain areas of difficulty and uncertainty which just happens to bring them power. Professionals do not passively receive knowledge which can then be applied to situations. The argument runs the other way. *Those who are in positions of power can control what situations mean and therefore can determine what knowledge is to be brought to bear on difficult situations.* Therapists actively create frameworks in which the family is to be understood. In the light of *their* definitions, they prescribe the changes which must take place in the family if proper functioning – again defined in their behavioural terms – is to be restored. Not only is knowledge power, but power determines what is to count as relevant knowledge. This reminds us that knowledge is created; it is a socially constructed phenomenon. It also reflects the interests of key social groups. 'Power,' writes Cohen (1985, p. 25), 'creates new objects of knowledge and accumulates new bodies of information.' In the arena of the 'social', the family occupies a special place and holds special social meaning. It has distinctive and highly significant properties. It is the site where the potential for public misconduct is constructed as well as the context in which it must be treated. The family therapist 'colonizes' the family in order to explore and explain why it has produced such patterns of behaviour. She is then in a position to remodel the way members relate so that conformity and social acceptability are re-established. The reshaping takes place along lines which reflect the thinking found in the domain of the social. Families are encouraged to alter their actions and interactions on the premiss that behavioural change is the true social reality and not some inner, self-absorbed, experiential state. In this world, control and treatment, punishment and cure are regular bedfellows. The one implies and entails the other as deviants are identified and rehabilitated, made fit once more to be full and useful members of society.

But power is rarely absolute and never permanent. Lukes (1974) recognized that the most effective and insidious form of power is to have others see things our way. In this most subtle guise, coercion is not necessary. 'Ideological hegemony' controls the thoughts and the minds of those under its sway. They learn to think and feel in ways which are socially appropriate. However, there will always be those who break out of such ideological straitjackets despite the soft lining that makes them feel comfortable and safe. Some people retain an ability to see things differently. They pose alternative realities and thus challenge the established bastions of power and the intellectual climate they sustain.

In their own modest way, the families whose experiences I have reported were a group who, in the main, felt uncomfortable with the reality being supplied by the therapists. They felt uneasy with a version of themselves that saw individual members only as parts of a systemic whole. Those who resisted family therapy in effect refused to recognize the right of the therapist to define and explain their situation. These small acts of defiance hint not only at an alternative knowledge base but also at a residue of power in those whose personal relationships have become objects of public scrutiny and interest. There are those who would wish to nurture this small remnant of power and help it grow. Those on the receiving end of health and welfare services, so the argument goes, have too little control over their own situation. Any personal social service worth its name should champion the clients' definition of their own needs and their own experiences. This model of family work demands that social workers listen to, and take note of, the consumer's view.

9 The personal and the political in family therapy

The voice of the consumer

There has persisted a good deal of curiosity about what social workers actually do. This has been reflected in studies which have described social workers, their practice and their clients. Raising the lid and peering inside the occupation has provided a useful portrait of the social worker and what she does. But descriptions of the practitioner and her practice lead to a second string of enquiries in which questions are posed such as 'Does what she does work? Is it effective?' These questions have been refined so many times that researchers of this persuasion are now more likely to ask 'Who does what to whom, when and with what effect?' 'What are the specific effects of specific interventions by specified therapists upon specific symptoms or patient types?' (Bergin, 1971, p. 245). Data take the form of measurable and quantifiable observations. For example, the researcher may ask how many times a week does Jane argue with her mother about staying out late at night or how often has Scott missed school this month? The style is that of the applied behavioural scientist on the look-out for causal relationships between one set of actions and another.

But should those who enquire about the social world progress in the manner of those who investigate the physical? The debates in sociology and psychology about whether the methods of the natural sciences were relevant to understanding people and their society led to a range of different research methods which eventually filtered through into social work. In its most simple form, the assertion was that people cannot be understood as if they were objects. People have free will, intentions and motives, and are in large measure agents of their own destiny. They have experiences and they hold views. Researchers and practitioners alike, if they are to understand other people, must appreciate how the world looks from the other's viewpoint. The shift is from measuring objectives to understanding subjectivities, from quantitative examinations to qualitative explorations, from the behavioural to the experiential.

In social work these methodological moves prompted the daring

97

idea of asking the clients of social work what they thought of the service which they had received. Rather than measure what changes could be observed in the client as the result of social work, consumers were asked for their views and experiences of welfare practices. What the client had to say became a valuable thing to hear; it was relevant to the way in which social workers should be judged and evaluated. Indeed, the position could be pushed further. The whole point of a personal service was to satisfy the users of that service. If they were not happy with the service received, it was up to social workers to change their practice in the light of the views expressed. The experiences of the consumer was the touchstone by which practice was to be judged:

> . . . an effective service requires us to know something about the responses and reactions of those we seek to help. (Sainsbury, 1975 p. 1)

> . . . our research practice of seeking accounts from clients *because the process of welfare intervention cannot be adequately understood without their views* represents for us a paradigm both for understanding and improving the services available to families in need . . . We would argue that any attempt to understand social work planning must take serious account of the views of the client and must analyse their proper role in the planning and delivery of services. (Fisher *et al.* 1986, pp. 4–5, emphasis original)

A steady flow of consumer-based research has washed into social work since the seminal study by Mayer and Timms (1970). On the whole, client satisfaction seems high, two-thirds of all users expressing some contentment with the service received. However, a number of commentators observe that a distinction has to be made between the client's view of the worker as a helpful person and the achievement of a useful outcome (for example, see Rees and Wallace, 1982). 'Ratings of satisfaction', records Fisher (1983, p. 42), cannot therefore be taken as a guide to the success of the service in meeting either its own goals or those of the client. Such measures relate primarily to the *quality* of the encounter between worker and client, not to its outcome.'

The family and its members has been a favourite target for consumer researchers. Not only those suffering material deprivations, but also those suffering interpersonal, behavioural and relationship problems have been asked for their views. Research findings in the area of interpersonal difficulties have been well rehearsed, but the main points are worth repeating (Craig 1981; Davies 1985; Fisher ed. 1983; Merrington and Corden 1981; Rees and Wallace 1982; Shaw 1984). There is a remarkable consistency in the findings, many of which are echoed in the present study. I shall review those which relate to families and their relationship problems under three headings: (i) feeling comfortable, (ii) making sense, and (iii) having a say.

Feeling comfortable

As well as comments about the suitability of the physical surroundings, the worker's personality, style and manner receive a good deal of comment from clients. The way it is done is at least as important as what is done. This dimension received early recognition in the immensely influential work of Truax and Carkhuff (1967). They believed that the theoretical flavour of the therapist was less important in terms of an effective outcome than her personal qualities, which included her attitude and manner. If she possessed the 'core conditions' of empathy, genuineness, and warmth, her clients were not only likely to enjoy the therapeutic experience, but they would probably be helped too. The person-centred therapies have taken these messages to heart. They value how the helper relates to the client more than what she does in technical terms. In other words, the quality of *being* is more important than the mechanics of *doing*.

Clients seek help in a condition of high anxiety. They are extra-sensitive to every nuance of their physical, emotional and interpersonal environment. They may be asking themselves 'Do I really want to be here?' Are these the people and is this the place for me to "open-up" and allow myself to be helped?' In order to confront their own feelings, clients have to feel relatively safe. Exposing difficult thoughts and emotions to both oneself and others requires a degree of trust and an atmosphere of care and understanding. Any aspect which threatens these feelings of trust and safety will cause the client to bring down the shutters, retracting those areas whose very vulnerability identifies them as in need of attention. Many of the views expressed by families who talked about 'becoming engaged' in the therapeutic process illustrate how sensitive people feel when asking for help. We heard how the method of treatment, the machines which were used to facilitate supervision, and the manner of the therapist all affected the families' experience of feeling helped. We also learned of the strong need to be understood, for the therapist to *listen* and to try and appreciate how members felt as individuals, as mothers and fathers, as well as a family unit.

Many studies find that the client's satisfaction increases if they like the worker and find the relationship to be a pleasant one. The quality of the encounter is taken to be an indication of whether or not the worker is interested in the client and his well-being.

Merrington and Corden's families spoke most enthusiastically about workers who were 'friendly, approachable people', 'the type of lady you could talk to' (1981, p. 225). Lishman (1978, p. 310) noted that clients who felt that they were valued and accepted were more likely to be satisfied. Sainsbury and Nixon (1979, p. 136) found that the social work service was 'equated with the personalities of the workers'. Rees and Wallace (1982, p. 29) observed that an 'unhurried approach' is especially appreciated by clients and, by way of illustration, quote from one of Rees's earlier interviews with a mother of a young mentally handicapped child: 'I was quite surprised they had the time to bother because they've lots of people to deal with and maybe my case, it was big to me, but it was quite trivial to them. But she was kind and could be bothered.' The emotional relief of having someone to talk to and someone to listen was a source of great comfort to many clients.

Making sense

'What's going on here?' is a question asked by participants in situations in which they need to find their bearings. Uncertainty is unnerving, confusion is disorientating. We seek to avoid these feelings by trying to make sense of what is happening. If this cannot be achieved, we become unsettled, we try to escape from the situation, or we attempt to rationalize that which seems to be without reason. There is a need to understand what is taking place. In Chapter 5 we met families who did feel that they could make sense of therapy and, as a result, they were able to understand what was happening to them as a family. But we also heard other families say that they could make 'neither head nor tail' of what the therapists were trying to do. The experience was 'weird' – much better to avoid it. They left therapy puzzled and angry.

Projection and fantasy are rife when few clues exist to explain what is going on. Merrington and Corden (1981, p. 254) reported that some of the families in their study 'seemed unsure and uncertain about what the workers thought', although others were willing to suspend judgement, trusting in the expertise of the therapists. Mrs A., recalling the occasion when the family was asked to construct a geneogram, said, 'I thought, "I don't see the point, but we'll go along with it." You have to accept the method they use at the clinic' (ibid, p. 253).

'Lack of agreement', observe Rees and Wallace (1982, p. 59), 'between client and social worker over the nature of the problem is one of the most important factors related to outcome.' Fisher *et al.* (1986, p. 53) found that 'Too often disagreements about the nature of problems and about methods of handling them remained unexplored undercurrents in the exchanges between workers and clients'. The most common bone of contention in family work is the insistence by parents that the problem is a particular child and that therefore the focus of treatment should be on that child and not the dynamics of the whole family, the state of the marriage or the pathology of interpersonal relations. For example, some of the clients of the Family Welfare Associaton in Mayer and Timms' study 'took for granted that the only way to improve the situation was to bring about changes in the offender's behaviour'. Sixteen years later, Fisher *et al.* (1986, p. 52) concluded: 'Where workers saw problems in relationships, clients, particularly parents, tended to see problems in people, a clash in perspective which led to fraught expectations and communication.' Shifting attention to the parents appears to induce feelings of self-blame and persecution. In turn, this provokes dissatisfaction and even rejection of the help given.

Many parents look for advice and guidance rather than diagnosis and treatment. 'I wanted to know what to do with him,' said one of Lishman's parents (1978, pp. 305–6), 'I wanted to be told I was doing right ... I wanted it pointed out what I was doing wrong.' Lishman found that in most of her twelve cases clients were unclear about what was happening while Shaw and Lebens (1977, p. 13), seeking the views of foster parents, went so far as to say that 'These foster parents and their social workers simply do not live in the same universe'. Similarly, dissatisfied clients who were looking for help with interpersonal problems in Mayer and Timms' study said they experienced a complete breakdown in communication because the workers did not explain to the clients what they were trying to achieve. The psychodynamic nature of the workers' practice mystified the families and formed an unbridgeable barrier.

Perhaps one of the most surprising and potentially devastating reports comes from the study conducted by Mary Ann Jones (1985). She looked at an experimental programme to prevent children in New York being received into foster care through the provision of intensive casework services to families at risk of breaking up. The research covers many aspects but one major finding was that the most successful practitioners at keeping children out of care and with their families were those who were the least professionally qualified – the 'non-MSWs'. These workers were less inclined to engage in highly technical, task-orientated, therapeutically intense styles of intervention. Instead, they were there when needed but set no deadlines or restrictions. They provided a 'medium to low intensity service', often delivered over several years.

'Perhaps,' reflects Jones (ibid, p. 143), 'we are seeing once again the greater importance of the sheer presence of a person . . . over the quality of the role performance brought to the job.' Just 'being there' and providing back up resources to families rather than enhancing interpersonal or even parental functioning' seem to be very important (ibid, p. 144). Whereas the more sophisticated techniques of the professional caseworkers remained a mystery to families, the less complicated presence of the non-MSW workers was understood; there was greater 'congruence' between the parents and these workers.

Having a say
More accurately views expressed under this heading are really to do with the balance of power between the worker and the client in that the more power one party holds, the greater is his or her ability to impose his or her definition of the situation. The key question here is 'Who is in control?' Clients generally like to have some control over the encounter, particularly when decisions are being made which affect them. Being party to decisions is seen as a key requirement if the relationship with the social worker is to be viewed in favourable terms. When clients feel powerless they grow resentful. Foster parents who are kept 'in the dark' about plans for their foster child cease to foster (Jones, 1985). Parents of mentally handicapped children who are not kept fully in the picture about their child feel dissatisfied (Robinson, 1978). Young people in care often feel uninvolved in the decisions which are taken which affect *their* lives (Fisher *et al.*, 1986; Reinach and Roberts, 1979). In contrast, methods which do require clients to explore and define their own problems and needs, as well as identify areas which they feel able to change, earn greater favour than techniques in which the expert's formulation of their problem condition is imposed – a formulation which may not even be divulged to the client.

Contradictions and ironies abound in this field. It is commonly found that families expect the 'expert' to give direct, authoritative advice: 'If they told us what to do so that we could put things right then, of course, we'd do it.' When direct advice is not forthcoming, the worker tends to be viewed critically. However, if the worker attempts to establish her expert view of the situation in a way which does not accord with the client's outlook, again she will be judged harshly. Social workers and therapists are most likely to succeed when the client either shares control or is quite happy to hand it over. These outcomes are most likely to happen when clients understand what is on offer, know what is going on and why, feel safe, believe they have relinquished control voluntarily, can comment on what is taking place, and, if necessary, can recover control if they so choose.

In 1987 Triseliotis warned that 'The uncritical adoption of "family therapy" models is likely to result in the kind of research findings identified by Mayer and Timms (1970) concerning work with individuals' (p. 9). I appear to be confirming the fears expressed in this warning. The consumer's view of therapy and family social work has generated a number of bold messages for practitioners. They cluster around two concepts which regularly excite the interest of social workers and which have been clearly visible throughout our review of consumer research: *subjectivity* and *power* or, as they are also known, the personal and the political. However, we need to examine them with a slightly keener eye to see if they are as wholesome and self-evidently straightforward as at first they appear.

Subjectivity

The concept of subjectivity encourages the belief that people can only be understood at the level of personal meaning. 'If social work thinking is not to fall into technocracy's de-personalising and de-humanising modes of reflection', believes Whan (1983, p. 323), 'it requires an appreciation of the person in his subjective and historical being.' Good practice demands that the worker tries to see the world from the client's point of view. Moreover, it is the client who is best placed to articulate his condition and consider what it means for him. Indeed, the claim is that an understanding of the other is not complete unless it takes into account his understanding and experience (ibid, p. 327). Techniques which involve the worker imposing her meanings on the actions of clients are alien to the person-centred approaches. The subjectivist helps fathom meaning. Meanings, though, can be changed. Unlike the worker who applies a therapeutic technique, the worker as humanist has no privileged outlook on how to view and interpret experiences. The therapist has to be in tune with her own feelings and she has to use her intuition if she is to engage the subjectivity of the other.

Clients want to be understood. 'Social work is always about the way people see things ... Any account of social work must therefore be based upon the meaning people give their experience' (England, 1986, p. 17). We constantly construct understandings of our world and the people in it. However, the crucial ingredient, at least as far as developing a critique of family therapy is concerned, is that only in the act of communication itself are understandings formulated. 'It is ... to everyman a matter of urgent personal importance to "describe" his experience, because this is literally a remaking of himself, a creative change in his personal organisation' (Williams, 1965, p. 42). This is never more so than when the individual is confused and puzzled, upset and at a loss what to do. It follows that techniques which stifle communication, or straitjacket and limit what can be said and described, frustrate understanding. In his elegant assault on family therapy, Whan develops this line of thought:

> The difficulty in any approach where the end may justify the means is that the means tend often to become an end in themselves. If one values human subjectivity, this necessarily includes self-understanding. Self-direction implies understanding as part of its reflective activity. If some means of creating change disavows the client's self-understanding, self-direction is curtailed as is subjectivity undermined. One is then advocating a way of relating to one's self and the selves of others through manipulation. The question posed is whether the social worker is prepared to go along with this 'technocratic' attitude towards subjectivity. (1983, pp. 334–5)

If communication helps families make sense of their experience and what it means, those who feel that their utterances are restricted to a special code called family therapy will fail to understand their own condition or make sense of the treatment process itself.

The therapist as humanist would not be surprised to learn that families were most critical of practitioners who were intent on *explaining* behaviour but neglected to *understand* personal experience. Family members want to be heard by the therapist which means that, first, she must learn to *listen*. But there is a prior phase: the stage of preparation. Families want to be prepared for the encounter, they want to understand the purpose of the method and the reasons for any equipment present. This stage has to be taken very slowly with the therapist showing great sensitivity. The therapeutic team has to earn the family's trust. In their comments, families were looking for a personal service. There is no place for supervisors who remain hidden and anonymous, no interest to be shown in techniques which are impersonal and unintelligible.

Power

When power is introduced into deliberations about the relationship between the producers and consumers of welfare services, it usually refers to the ability of one party to define matters to suit its interests. Clearly, many consumers feel that they have too little power in their dealings with health and welfare experts. In areas of critical importance, users feel unable to influence what is taking place. The definition of the problem and the explanation of its cause lie outside their control. Actions designed to tackle the situation are determined by the worker. Often the nature of these actions or the reasons for using them are not discussed with clients. The only power clients have, at least in voluntary encounters, is to reject the service and this, as we have seen, is what many of them do. Roth (1973) calls this 'the right to quit'. However, if note is taken of the consumer's view, the implications for practice are clear. Clients should have a greater say in what happens to them. The balance of power should shift in their direction. They should become more involved in the process of defining the problem, explaining its origins and determining the manner of its resolution. Out of such findings have emerged a group of closely related ideas: empowerment of the client, shared control and participation. Each is based on the proposition that the personal social services should take account of the client's view of the situation. Indeed, they go further and argue that the client has a right to influence the way in which the situation is defined and to have a say in what actions are to be taken. The practitioner is no longer the sole arbiter of what is to be done: large slices of control are handed back to the client. This is taken to be not only a sign of good and fair practice, but a reflection of what the nature of the relationship between the state and welfare clients should be. Not only should 'the voices of the clients themselves be heard in research findings', but, continue Fisher *et al.*, family policy should regard families 'as active participants with cogent views which might change policy' (1986, p. 4). Social work planning should take serious account of the views of the client (ibid., p. 5).

Such recommendations are part of the broader assault on the power of both the state and the professions. Professions are seen as occupational groups which have established control over key areas of everyday life. Illich (1977) sees the professions as a form of domination by technology. Professional groups determine how work should be done and by whom it shall be done. They also decide what services shall be produced and for whom they are appropriate. The archetypal professions dominate the relationship with the client. They define the needs of the consumer *and* the manner in which these needs are to be met (Johnson, 1972).

Illich is one of the most trenchant critics of the professions, regarding them as occupational groups that have gradually and inexorably wrested control from, and undermined, the competence of those who are now in receipt of their expert services. Doctors and architects, teachers and social workers have taken away the ability of people to learn to help themselves in basic areas of personal and social living. They are the 'disabling professions.' As a result, people are less able to cope with the ordinary problems of their day-to-day lives. He feels that professions have eaten into almost every corner of modern life. Writing about education, Illich proclaims: 'The mere existence of school discourages and disables the poor from taking control of their own learning. All over the world the school has an anti-educational effect on society: school is recognised as the institution which specialises in education' Illich, 1973, p. 75). Wilding (1982, p. 113) expands on those observations and suggests that three points are being made.

1. The existence of specialized educational institutions means that people are discouraged from pursuing their own education.
2. Because school is presumed to be the only place where education occurs, no effort is made to develop the educative possibilities of ordinary life.
3. It is suggested that the educational process is a difficult business and cannot be realistically pursued except under professional guidance.

Teachers act in place of parents rather than *with* them. And what is true for education is equally true of medicine and welfare. People are denied the responsibility for their own condition and its treatment. They become dependent on the alleged expertise of others. Instead of coping with their difficult offspring or caring for their frail relatives, families despair and turn to the professionals. People became clients and they fall into passivity. But Wilding concludes his review with these comments:

> Clearly professions can and do enable as well as disable, but enabling depends on an egalitarian philosophy and the sharing of power and knowledge between professional and client. Preservation of the power, prestige and privileges of the professions depends, or seems to depend, on the maintenance of a decent gulf between professionals and clients. Such a gulf is an important element in the disabling situation and it is an inevitable corollary of the paternal model of professional work, where the professional confronts his client from a position of distant superiority rather than equality. Professionals can start from where people are, building on their capacity to help themselves or they can confront those who seek their services with their own professional definition of the problem which substantially ignores the views and capacities of the person seeking help. (ibid,. p. 117)

The banner call that arises out of these criticisms is for the return of large measures of control to those who use the health and welfare services. We recognize it in the ideas of 'patch-based' social work where practitioners are encouraged to develop the self-helping capacities of the community. It is present in aspects of task-centred casework with its insistence on helping the client identify his own problems and explore ways in which these might be tackled. The central theme is that of a *partnership* between the consumer and the producer. Partnership means sharing information. It entails explaining to the user what is going on. And, in its most radical guise, it demands that power is shared with the client and that users are fully involved in the making of all significant decisions.

Maluccio *et al.* (1986) have pioneered a good deal of this type of thinking in the field of child care and family work. They endorse the belief that parents should become full partners in the helping process. Parents should see themselves as resources to be used on their own behalf. Maluccio himself insists that we shift from a pathological view of parents to one in which they are seen as potentially competent performers. In short, parents should be *empowered*.

In her report on how and why decisions are made about admitting children into care, Packman (1986) provides a detailed picture of prevailing child care services. Her research method relied heavily upon the subjective judgements of social workers and the parents of children who were being considered for care. Again, what emerges is that practice was often based on a crude, narrow and leaden interpretation of policy. The effect of this was to devalue and ignore the views and experiences of the parents. The aim, in many cases, was simply to keep children out of care even when admission may have been a positive and appropriate response. Parents 'were apparently as likely to find admission helpful as otherwise, not only for their own sakes, but for children's as well' (Packman, 1986, p. 197). She concludes:

> Statements that assert that 'admission to care should be a last resort' or that 'it is to be prevented at all costs', and policies which equate low admission rates with good child care, for example, seem to us singularly unhelpful – yet they were much in evidence in departmental documents and in discussions with staff at many levels. Detailed guidance as to what kinds of admission are best avoided and how prevention might be achieved, and suggestions about what admissions may actually be beneficial, and why, might be of more use. (ibid., p. 197).

Partnership and empowerment appear in strong measure in the conclusion reached by Fisher *et al.* (1986). Having reported on the 'care' experiences of children, parents and social workers, the authors came down heavily in favour of a partnership between public agencies and families. Families should retain their primary caring role although they may choose to work in tandem with the state at critical stages. This might be termed 'assisted parenting (ibid., p. 131). Policy is pulled away from promoting social work roles which are controlling and interventionist towards ones which value the development of a cooperative relationship with families. The family is turned from a liability into a resource. However, in this remodelled practice, a child's entry into care is not perceived as a failure. The message from parents is that short periods in care with continued contact with home is an acceptable formulation for dealing with troublesome children. This emphasizes the need for social workers to take the parents' point of view seriously. Rather than resist care at all costs, social workers might think about it more positively and constructively, as part of an agreed strategem between the parents, the child and the worker. Throughout, there is an emphasis on keeping all parties informed of what is happening. The views of all participants must be sought and introduced into the discussions and decisions which take place. 'The common factor, if a partnership approach is to be adopted, is that participants should be able to call for an account of what is going on, with whom and with what aims. They should feel that they have a right to this account' (Fisher *et al.*, 1986, p. 140).

This version of empowerment takes the slightly softer line. Clients are kept informed of what is happening. Their views are sought. But their ability to control events remains limited or, at best, lies with the discretion of the worker. The stronger version gives parents and children direct control over how their problem is to be understood and how resources might be deployed to help them cope with their situation. Discussions about the extent to which parents should participate in childcare case conferences have explored much of this ground. How much power is to be shared becomes the crunch issue. McGloin and Turnbull (1986 p. 9) quote two authors who recommend an increase in consumer power. They demonstrate the various interpretations that can be given to the concept of participation. First the weak version given by Phillips:

> Effective parental participation has been achieved when the parents understand the process that they are going through and both they and the professionals feel that they have made a useful contribution to the plan of action.

Gostin prefers a slightly stronger stance:

> The term 'client participation' means that departments share the decisions they take with those people who are to be affected by them. Meaningful participation requires that they be provided with all the information available to the department ... It also requires that the person to be affected by a decision is invited to case conferences to put

his view and, where the individual feels vulnerable and unable to present his case effectively, he should be given the opportunity of being represented.

However, it is possible to shift the axis of power even further towards the user. This brings us back to Illich where he is joined by many of social work's radical practitioners. They go beyond any simple ideas of power-sharing, suggesting that clients should recover control over how their difficulties are defined and that they should determine the kind of services and resources that should be available to meet their needs. This not only removes all power from the expert to define other people's problems, but also denies the expert the right to impose a particular treatment response. Instead, the worker becomes a resource, a means to someone else's end. The conventional stance is turned inside out. Control and responsibility over day-to-day life and its problems are returned to the individual, the family and the community.

Social work with families

All this is very provocative. For some it is politically extreme; for others it is romantic nonsense. But, again, we are left to wonder how far, if at all, a systemic family therapist can take ideas of participation and empowerment and still remain a systemic family therapist. Consumer studies and radical humanistic analyses conclude that the client is short on power, lacks control and lies passive before the might of the therapist. The prescription is based on a phenomenological critique of the idea that members of an occupational group become experts in the personal affairs of other people.

The weaker version of partnership could be absorbed by systemic family therapy, at least to some degree. Therapists *could* explain the basis on which they understand family life without losing impact. They *could* divulge that analysing the pattern of interpersonal relationships casts a penetrating light on the way families behave. Many books on 'how to practise family therapy' do contain firm advice on the need to explain to families the systemic nature of the worker's practice. Burnham (1986), for example, is quite clear on this. Therapists should give families an introduction to family therapy. This should include information about how sessions are conducted and a positive rationale for the method chosen. The worker should explain who she is, the reasons and value of live supervision and any technical equipment used, and the benefits of meeting the whole family. Burnham then quotes the introduction that he and his colleagues at the Charles Burns Clinic give to families at their first session:

Hello, as I said in reception my name is X. To start with I would like to explain the way in which we work [pause]. I work as part of a team, and my colleagues are sitting behind this [gesturing], which is a one-way screen. They watch the way in which I work in order to help me to help you. From time to time they may knock on the door to call me out of the room, so that we can share our opinions. I may also choose to go out [pause]. We make a videotape-recording of the session, using those two cameras that you can see [gesturing]. This is so that I don't need to take notes and can pay full attention to what you have to say. I look through the tape in between sessions to work out what is the best way to proceed [pause]. We have a consent form which explains your safeguards about the confidentiality of the information on the videotape. I'll give you the form later in the session. I'd like you to read through it and sign it if you are in agreement. (Burnham, 1986, pp. 108–9)

However it must be emphasized that although the therapist explains the nature and purpose of her techniques and remains courteous and sensitive to the family's anxieties, not for one moment does she concede any of her real power. The basis on which the family's behaviour is to be explained and the techniques to be used lie entirely in the hands of the therapist. Systemic family therapy is not a framework designed to accommodate alternative definitions of the way the family system functions. Indeed, why should it? Although from the point of view of the democratic humanist this is taken as a weakness, from the position of the therapeutic technician it is an undoubted strength.

But there are many who have sought to soften the hard line of the purist. They have listened to families and, though not necessarily renouncing all systemic and structural thoughts, they have taken note of the consumer's voice. Will and Wrate (1985), for example, feel that structural family therapy on its own is inflexible. Indeed, pure models of family therapy tend to be prompted by evangelists who want nothing to do with other schools of thought. Will and Wrate believe this view to be narrowminded. In its stead, they have developed an 'integrated' approach to family therapy. They weave together elements of behavioural and psychoanalytic, systemic and structural theories and techniques. It has to be noted that all these contributory theories have a broadly scientific and 'functionalist' orientation, but the net result is a model of practice that shows diversity and variety. The authors describe themselves as 'closet eclectics'. In particular, they meld methods which value families working in the 'here and now' on tasks and current experiences in order to explore what is happening *and* the use of interpretation (derived from psychoanalysis) leading to insight. But the therapists require the families' cooperation.

Indeed, Will and Wrate pride themselves on working 'collaboratively' with the family:

> It is important to establish a spirit of collaborative and open enquiry with the family. The family should be greeted and settled down and provided with some idea of the nature of the interview to follow . . . . The therapist then proceeds to clarify why family members think they are at the session, what they expect will happen and what they hope will come out of it. . . . The therapist should then summarize and feed back his perception of the family's views about the purpose of the assessment and should then outline his own views of the purpose of this meeting, in particular making it clear why he has asked all family members to attend. . . . (1985, pp. 36–7)

> Problem clarification: This refers to the therapist obtaining partial or complete agreement between himself and the family about the problems that have emerged as being significant during the assessment. . . . By the end of the interview, the therapist should have established to what extent he and the family have been able to develop a mutually acceptable definition of what the problems are. . . . (1985, pp. 42–3)

Even so, much of the power to define, explain and treat remains with the therapist. When the theoretical atmosphere still conjures the practitioner as expert, the client's voice, though heard, is subdued.

Will and Wrate take firm steps towards the consumer but, a few strides further on, we meet Murgatroyd and Woolfe (1985). They call themselves helpers rather than therapists. Again, they raid behaviourism and psychoanalysis as well as the mainstream family therapies for their ideas. But they still believe that the individual can only be understood in the context of the family system: '. . . the "needs" presented by an individual within a family arise from the nature of the family's communication and interactions systems and it is this that the helper needs to focus upon if he or she is to reduce distress within the family' (ibid., p. 5). The authors prefer to call their model 'family focused helping'. They describe their theoretical position as 'humanist and pragmatic', although, as I have argued, allying humanism with even the remnants of objectivism is an unlikely achievement. Nevertheless, Murgatroyd and Woolfe believe that the helper must attend to feelings and thoughts, as well as behaviour, in each family member (1985, p. 120). There is an emphasis on 'the helper examining the way in which family members understand their situation, the ways in which they seek to cope with it and the meaning they attribute to their own coping. The aim is that the helper should come to understand this experience in the context of the coping strategy adopted by the family and its members' (ibid., p. 132). The authors recommend plentiful use of empathy, genuineness and warmth. Their eventual recipe reads as follows:

> The successful use of these procedures and processes is . . . dependent upon the quality of the helper's relationships with the individuals and the family with whom they are working. This relationship will need to involve: (a) a sensitivity on the part of the helper to the feelings and concerns of the family . . .; (b) the helper explaining to the family members with whom he or she is working the rationale for the procedures used so that they do not feel manipulated, used or exploited; (c) the helper seeking to build trust and show concern both between him- or herself and the family members and also between the family members themselves; (d) the helper being genuine in his or her transactions with those who he or she seeks to help . . .; (e) the helper needing to be 'concrete' – meaning that he or she should be seen to be working with the specific problems and concerns of the family, and finally (f) the helper needing to show warmth and empathy to those who seek his or her help. (Murgatroyd and Woolfe, 1985, p. xv).

I think that Murgatroyd and Woolfe go as far as anyone can and still remain on speaking terms with the unadulterated family therapist. They offer an attractive blend of techniques. Focused family helping pays its respect to the subjectivity of the other. It makes a gesture towards empowering the family. But so long as its proponents continue to gain some inspiration from approaches which are systemic and scientific, there is an in-built limit to how far they can travel down the road of subjectivity and client empowerment. For many social workers, focused family helping would seem to offer a wholesome package, combining the best of family therapy with a sufficient concern for the personal experience of the consumer and his or her wish for some control over proceedings.

Beyond this point, we leave mainline family therapy behind and enter what many social work writers call simply 'working with families'. Triseliotis offers a useful review of this position. He contends 'that the techniques of classical "family therapy" are too narrow to be applicable to more than a few families seen by social workers in social services (work) departments' (1987, p. 6). However, once the worker rejects the theoretical obligations of classical family therapy, he or she is free to respond to the messages which emerge from the consumer and his or her experience. The idea of 'personal meaning' and notions of empowerment sit more comfortably with the concept of 'working with families'. This position is not derived from theoretical principles, but is based on a moral stance founded on the pragmatism and expediency that saturate the daily workings of social work departments. In other words, the relationship between the worker and the family is not technologically led. It is ideologically sponsored. I have already mentioned Maluccio, Packman and Fisher *et al*. Their conclusions give added support to practices of this kind and, clearly, their insistence that more power and control be given to clients gives such ideas a distinctly radical flavour.

Conclusion

We have gone as far as we can, and a bit further, within the confines of family therapy and its critique. The reasoning that brings us to this conclusion has been as follows.

The theoretical assumptions that inform the practice of family therapy on the one hand, and the qualitative research enquiries on the other, differ. What each sees and values differs. The language that each uses employs a different vocabulary. It is difficult for one practice to speak to the other without sounding rude and dismissive. If the practitioner chooses to listen to the client, she is siting herself in a particular epistemological arena which values and promotes the subjectivity of the other.

Thus, if practice is to be influenced by the views of the consumer, it is doubtful whether the practitioner can give herself over entirely to classical family therapy. Therapists, including systemic family therapists, offer a theoretical framework which explains all family behaviour in prescribed conceptual terms. These terms include any views expressed by family members on the therapeutic experience. To accept these views as behaviours which can be located outside the framework of therapeutic understanding is to undermine the logic of the framework itself. The only consistent position to adopt, if the consumer's view is to be accepted and acted upon, is to assert a different framework – one which takes the individual's experience as the basis of social theorizing. Researchers and practitioners who pursue the client's view as a perspective which should inform practice make this kind of understanding. 'Working with families' allows practitioners to be influenced by the consumer's experience. Therefore a practice such as 'working with families' has built into its own developmental logic notions of client subjectivity and consumer empowerment.

In its own terms, family therapy is consistent and self-reflexive, intellectually penetrating and professionally potent. In choosing to wander outside these terms, I may be forfeiting my ability to talk to systemic family therapists but, in so doing, I hope to open up another conversation between the client and the family social worker.

Appendix

Letter sent to family from Social Services Department

Address

date

Dear

I am writing to you because you have recently had some contact with social workers from the Social Services Department. The Department is interested in improving the service it gives to families. We are at present co-operating with an independent researcher from the University of East Anglia, Dr David Howe, in a study of the opinions and views of those who have used our services. I am, therefore, writing to ask if you would help by permitting the research worker to interview your family in your own home to obtain your views about the service you received.

Any information you provide will be treated in strictest confidence. Your name will not be used in any way, nor will anyone in the Social Services Department or anywhere else be able to connect your name with anything you have said. It is only in this way that we can hope to obtain frank answers from the persons interviewed.

A fee of £5 will be offered by the research institute in return for your time and co-operation and will be paid when the interview takes place. Dr Howe would like to contact you to arrange a convenient time for him to visit you and your family. If I do not hear from you to the contrary by   (date)   I shall assume that you would like him to call.

Thanking you in anticipation.

Yours sincerely,

Divisional Manager

(Adapted from Mayer and Timms, 1970, p. 151)

Bibliography

Ackerman, N. W. (1958), *The Psychodynamics of Family Life*, New York: Basic Books.

Aponte, Harry J. and VanDeusen, John M. (1981), 'Structural family therapy' in A. S. Gurman and David P. Kniskern (eds.), *Handbook of Family Therapy*, New York: Brunner/Mazel.

Bateson, G., Jackson, D., Haley, J. and Weakland, J. (1956), 'Towards a Theory of Schizophrenia', *Behavioural Science*, 1, p. 251.

Bergin, A. (1971), 'The evaluation of therapeutic outcomes' in A. Bergin and S. Garfield (eds.), *Handbook of Psychotherapy Behaviour Change*, New York: Wiley.

Broderick, Carlfred B. and Schrader, Sandra S. (1981), 'The history of professional marriage and family therapy' in A. S. Gurman and D. P. Kniskern (eds.), *Handbook of Family Therapy*, New York: Brunner/Mazel.

Bulmer, Martin (1979), 'Concepts in the analysis of qualitative data', *Sociological Review*, 27(4), pp. 651–77.

Burnham, John B. (1986), *Family Therapy: first steps towards a systemic approach*, London: Tavistock.

Burrell, G. and Morgan, G. (1979), *Sociological Paradigms and Organisational Analysis*, London: Heinemann.

Cade, B. W. (1984), 'Paradoxical techniques in therapy', *Journal of Child Psychology and Psychiatry*, 25, pp. 509–16.

The Child, the Family and the Young Offender, Cmnd. 2742, Aug. 1965.

Cohen, Stanley (1985), *Visions of Social Control*, Cambridge: Polity Press.

Craig, G. (1981), *Review of Studies of the Public and Users' Attitudes, Opinions and Expressed Needs with Respect to Social Work and Social Workers*, London: National Institute for Social Work.

Davies, Martin (1985), *The Essential Social Worker*, Aldershot: Gower

Davis, Kathy (1986), 'The process of problem (re)formulation in psychotherapy', *Sociology of Health and Illness*, 8(1), March, pp. 44–74.

Donzelot, Jacques (1979), *The Policing of Families*, London: Hutchinson.

England, Hugh (1986), *Social Work as Art: making sense for good practice*, London: Allen and Unwin.

Fisher, Mike (ed.) (1983), *Speaking of Clients*, Sheffield: Joint Unit for Social Services Research, University of Sheffield.

Fisher, Mike (1983), 'The meaning of client satisfaction', in M. Fisher (ed.) *Speaking of Clients*, Sheffield: University of Sheffield.

Fisher, Mike, Marsh, Peter and Phillips, David (1986), *In and Out of Care: the experiences of children, parents and social workers*, London: Batsford.

Glaser, B. G. and Straus, A. L. (1967), *The Discovery of Grounded Theory*, Chicago: Aldine.

Gorrell Barnes, G. (1984), *Working with Families*, London: Macmillan.

Gould, A. (1980), 'The salaried middle class in the corporatist welfare state', *Policy and Politics*, **9**.

Gurman, Alan S. and Kniskern, David P. (eds.) (1981), *Handbook of Family Therapy*, New York: Brunner/Mazel.

Haley, J. (1971), 'A review of the family therapy field' in J. Haley (ed.), *Changing Families*, New York: Grune and Stratton.

Harris, Robert and Webb, David (1987), *Welfare, Power, and Juvenile Justice*, London: Tavistock.

Howe, David (1986), *Social Workers and Their Practice in Welfare Bureaucracies*, Aldershot: Gower.

Howe, David (1988), 'A framework for understanding evaluation studies in social work', *Research, Policy and Planning*, **5(2)**.

Illich, I. (1973), *Deschooling Society*, London: Penguin.

Illich, Ivan (1977), *Limits to Medicine*, London: Penguin.

Ingleby Report (1960), *Report of the Committee on Children and Young Persons*, London: HMSO.

Johnson, Harriette C. (1986), 'Emerging concerns in family therapy', *Social Work*, July–August, pp. 299–306.

Johnson, Terence J, (1972), *Professions and Power*, London: Macmillan.

Jones, Mary Ann (1985), *A Second Chance for Families*, New York: Child Welfare League of America.

Kritzeck, James (1964), *Anthology of Islamic Literature*, New York: Holt, Rinehart and Winston, p. 217.

Lasch, Christopher (1977), *Haven in a Heartless World*, New York: Basic Books.

Lishman, Joyce (1978), 'A clash in perspective?', *British Journal of Social Work*, **8(3)**, pp. 301–11.

Lukes, Steven (1974), *Power: A Radical View*, London: Macmillan.

McGloin, Paul and Turnbull, Annmarie (1986), *Parent Participation in Child Abuse Review Conferences*, Greenwich: Greenwich Social Services.

Maluccio, Anthony N., Fein, Edith and Olmstead, Kathleen A. (1986), *Permanency Planning for Children*, London: Tavistock.

Manor, Oded (ed.) (1984), *Family Work in Action: a handbook for social workers*, London, Tavistock.

Masson, Helen C. and O'Byrne, Patrick (1984), *Applying Family Therapy: a practical guide for social workers*, Oxford: Pergamon Press.

Mayer, John and Timms, Noel (1970), *The Client Speaks*, London: Routledge and Kegan Paul.

Merrington, Diana and Corden, John (1981), 'Families' impressions of family therapy', *Journal of Family Therapy*, 3, pp. 243–61.

Millham, S. *et al.* (1986), *Lost in Care*, Aldershot: Gower.

Minuchin, S. and Fishman, C. (1981), *Family Therapy Techniques*, Cambridge, Mass: Harvard University Press.

Morgan, D. H. J. (1985), *The Family, Politics and Social Theory*, London: Routledge and Kegan Paul.

Murgatroyd, Stephen and Woolfe, Ray (1985), *Helping Families in Distress*, London: Harper and Row.

Nuttall, Kathryn (1985), *The Place of Family Therapy in Social Work*, Norwich: Social Work Monographs, University of East Anglia.

Packman, Jean (1986), *Who Needs Care? Social-Work Decisions about Children*, Oxford: Blackwell.

Pearson, G. (1974), 'Prisons of love: the reification of the family in family therapy' in N. Armstead (ed.), *Reconstructing Social Psychology*, Harmondsworth: Penguin.

Poster, Mark (1978), *Critical Theory of the Family*, London: Pluto Press.

Rees, Stuart and Wallace, Alison (1982), *Verdicts on Social Work*, London: Edward Arnold.

Reinach, E. and Roberts, G. (1979), *Consequences*, Milldam Barracks, Portsmouth: Social Services Research and Intelligence Unit.

Renner, K. (1953), 'Wandlungen der modernen Gesellschaft, Vienna', quoted in A. Giddens and G. Mackenzie (eds.) (1982), *Social Class and the Division of Labour*, Cambridge: Cambridge University Press.

Robinson, T. (1978), *In Worlds Apart*, London: Bedford Square Press.

Rojek, Chris (1986), The 'subject' in social work', *British Journal of Social Work*, **16(1)**, pp. 65–77.

Roth, J. A. (1973), 'The right to quit', *Sociological Review*, **23(3)**.

Sainsbury, Eric (1975), *Social Work with Families*, London: Routledge and Kegan Paul.

Sainsbury, E. and Nixon, S. (1979), 'Organisational influences on the ways in which social work practice is perceived by social workers and clients'. Sheffield: University of Sheffield.

Seebohm Report (1968), *Report of the Committee on Local Authority and Allied Personal Social Services*, London: Cmnd, 3703, HMSO.

Shaw, Ian (1984), 'Literature, review: consumer evaluations of the personal social services', *British Journal of Social Work*, **14(3)**, pp. 277–84.

Shaw, M. and Lebens, K. (1977), 'Foster parents talking', *Adoption and Fostering*, **88(2)**, pp. 11–16.

Stanton, M. Duncan (1981), 'Strategic approaches to family therapy' in Alan S. Gurman, Alan S. and David P. Kniskern (eds.) *Handbook of Family Therapy*, New York: Brunner/Mazel.

Triseliotis, John (1987), '"Family therapy" or working with families', *Practice*, **1(1)**, pp. 5–13.

Truax, C. B. and Carkhuff, R. R. (1967), *Towards Effective Counselling, and Psychotherapy*, Chicago: Aldine.

Vernon, J. and Fruin, D. (1986), *In Care: a case study of social work decision making*, London: National Children's Bureau.

Walrond-Skinner, S. (1977), *Family Therapy: the treatment of natural systems*, London: Routledge and Kegan Paul.

Watzlawick, P., Weakland, J. and Fisch, R. (1974), *Change: principles of problem formation and problem resolution*, New York: Norton.

Whan, Michael (1983), 'Tricks of the trade: questionable theory and practice in family therapy', *British Journal of Social Work*, **13(3)**, pp. 321–37.

Wilding, Paul (1982), *Professional Power and Social Welfare*, London: Routledge and Kegan Paul.

Will, David and Wrake, Robert M. (1985), *Integrated Family Therapy*, London: Tavistock.

Williams, R. (1965), *The Long Revolution*, Harmondsworth: Penguin.

Zastrow, Charles (1984), 'Understanding and preventing burn-out', *British Journal of Social Work*, **14(2)**, pp. 141–51.

Zuk, G. H. (1978), 'Value conflict in today's family', *Marriage and Family Living*, **60**, pp. 18–20.

Index